DRINKING
BOSTON

ALSO BY STEPHANIE SCHOROW

Boston on Fire: A History of Firefighting in Boston

The Cocoanut Grove Fire

The Crime of the Century:
How the Brink's Robbers Stole Millions and the
Hearts of Boston

East of Boston: Notes from the Harbor Islands

The Boston Mob Guide: Hitmen, Hoodlums and
Hangouts, with Beverly Ford

Boston's Fire Trail, editor

DRINKING
BOSTON

A HISTORY OF THE CITY AND ITS SPIRITS

STEPHANIE SCHOROW

Boston  UNION PARK PRESS

Union Park Press
Wellesley, MA 02481
www.unionparkpress.com

Printed in U.S.A.
First Edition

© 2012 Union Park Press

Library of Congress Cataloging-in-Publication Data

Schorow, Stephanie.
  Drinking Boston : a history of the city and its spirits / Stephanie Schorow.
      p. cm.
  Includes bibliographical references and index.
  ISBN 978-1-934598-09-2 (pbk.)
  1. Drinking of alcoholic beverages--Massachusetts--Boston--History. 2. Bars
(Drinking establishments)--Massachusetts--Boston--History.
  3. Prohibition--Massachusetts--Boston. 4. Alcoholic beverages--Massachusetts-
-Boston--History. 5. Boston (Mass.)--Social life and customs. I. Title.
  HV5298.B7D75 2012
  364.1'30974461—dc23
                                        2012036290

  ISBN: 978-1-934598-09-2

Book and cover design by Holly Gordon. www.missgordon.com

Cover: Boston Celebrates Repeal Night, December 5, 1933.
Courtesy of the Trustees of the Boston Public Library.

Union Park Press titles are also available in a variety of digital formats.
Please visit our website to learn more: www.unionparkpress.com

To my mother and father for teaching moderation and exuberance.

TABLE *of* CONTENTS

Scollay Square, 1957. © Massachusetts Institute of Technology.
Courtesy of MIT Libraries, Rotch Visual Collections;
Photograph by Nishan Bichajian.

ACKNOWLEDGMENTS

Unsurprisingly, lots of people volunteered to "help" me with my "research" on *Drinking Boston*. In addition to these companions along the bar, there were so many others who were extremely generous with their time and expertise, and I will always be grateful for their help.

In no particular order, I want to thank Brother Cleve, Jackson Cannon, Patrick Sullivan, Misty Kalkofen, Alexei Beratis, John Gertsen, Jamie Walsh, Ron Della Chiesa, Jerry Burke, Eddie Burke, Jerry Foley, Leo Motsis, Roger Sampson, Sarah-Ann Shaw, Michael Reiskind, Devin Hahn, Luke O'Neil, David Kruh, Robert Davis Sullivan, Libby Bouvier, Thomas Richardson, Greg Rossi, and the many bartenders and mixologists who introduced me to the joys of a well-made cocktail. Ronald Arntz and his mother, Rose Arntz, helped fill me in on the nightclubs of the 1930s; Rose also showed me that grace and beauty has no age limit. I'm very thankful to Edith Nussinow who spoke so eloquently about her father, Jacques Renard. Yet again, I am indebted to Kathy Alpert of Postmark Press for her fantastic knowledge of ephemera and her overwhelming generosity. I wish to thank Jane Winton, Henry Scannell, and all of the excellent staff of the Boston Public Library, Jeanne Gamble and the folks at Historic New England, the Massachusetts Historical Society, and the History Project, as well as the staff of the *Boston Herald* and *Boston Globe*. Also thanks to William Sheehan,

Margaret Sullivan, Laurie Cabot, Heidi Webb, Adele Maestranzi, Joyce McCann Kingston, Frederic Yarm, Connie Dodge, Anne Gallagher, Kimberly Whitaker of the West End Museum, Mary Eng, and my beloved, beautiful goddaughter Stephanie Cross for her research help. A special shout-out goes to my partner-in-mob-crime Beverly Ford for her crucial help at a crucial time and to readers Renee DeKona and Tom Nutile. I wish I could mention everyone who has helped me along the way, including bookstores, library staff, and eBay vendors who helped me find some of the artwork that you see in this book.

Most of all, I wish to sincerely thank Union Park Press publisher Nicole Vecchiotti who first proposed the book and who nurtured and nudged the author with never-flagging enthusiasm and patience. Without her excellent suggestions and overall direction, this book would not have been possible. The crew at Union Park Press has been fantastic: Shelby Larsson, Caitlin Cullerot, Holly Gordon, and Madeline Williams. I am extremely grateful for the copyediting and suggestions from Christopher Klein. Many thanks go to intern Jane Domino who fearlessly performed tedious research. And lastly, I have to thank *Drink Boston* blogger Lauren Clark for her friendship, encouragement, and expert advice. Lauren, this Bud's for you.

One last note: The author is well aware of the danger of alcoholism. She has seen, first hand, the effect of alcohol addiction on good friends and family. (Brian C: All is forgiven.) This book is not intended to minimize the health risks of alcoholism or to undercut the efforts of those who choose not to drink. Alcoholism is a deadly disease that affects both drinkers and those around them. So a final thought goes out to all the friends of Bill W. I wish you strength for the journey.

HENDRICKS CLUB, BOSTON'S FAMOU[S] DEMOCRATIC ORGANIZATION.

JOSEPH P. LOMASNEY BROTHERS Ist LIEUT

HON. MARTIN M. LOMASNEY

HENDRICKS CLUB OCCUPIES TWO UPPER STORIES ❋ SHOWS OFFICE OF M.M.LOMASNEY

HON. M.M. LOMASNEY'S POLITICAL STAFF.

BUILDING AND ROOMS OF CLUB NOVEMBER 1884 TO JULY 1908

HON. THOS. A. HENDRICKS WHOS MEMORY THE CLUB HONORS

HENDRICKS MEN IN CITY AND STATE
McCURDY   SONNABEND   MANCOVITZ
CUDDY   WHELTON   HART

INTRODUCTION: RECIPE FOR A DRINKING TOWN

The Ward Eight looms large in the mythical history of mixology, wherein it stands tall as the Champion of the Hub, proving to one and all that when Boston was called upon to contribute a Cocktail to the great pageant of American intoxication, it did not say, "I shall not serve."

—David Wondrich, *Imbibe! From Absinthe Cocktail to Whiskey Smash*

The chilled cocktail glass is set on the bar, beaded with drops of water, rosy with promise. Sip. The whiskey rolls over your tongue, the lemon juice and grenadine lining up just behind. The drink is the color of a blush or the last hurrah of a fading sunset. It is not a drink to be hurried.

This is the Ward Eight, a cocktail that is one part history, one part myth, and all parts Boston. If the Freedom Trail symbolizes the American Revolution and if the Green Monster says "Red Sox," then the Ward Eight cocktail represents Boston's drinking history: its spirit of invention, its hardscrabble politics, its mythology, and even the Hub's never-ending battle between personal freedom and civic reform.

That is a lot to fit in one cocktail glass. And in that way, the Ward Eight is like Boston, with so much history, culture, and traffic packed into such a small space.

Take another sip. Recall an old Boston political slogan: "Never write if you can speak; never speak if you can nod; never nod if you can wink." Martin Michael Lomasney allegedly said that. Martin Lomasney, who ranks with Mayor James Michael Curley—the infamous "Rascal King"—as one of Boston's canniest politicians at the turn of the last century. Lomasney, dubbed the "Boston Mahatma," ran Ward 8 in Boston's West End with a mix of street smarts and compassion. Whether in or out of elective office, Lomasney was a master of Boston's gritty politics.

Sip again. Let your mind wander back in time to 1898. Picture yourself sitting in Boston's Locke-Ober Café, a venerable eating establishment in Boston's downtown, once considered one of the city's finest dining spots. It is the night before Election Day, and a political club is gathered at the Ober bar awaiting victory. (Yes, a victory foretold.) The Hendricks Club, a political organization founded by Lomasney, is celebrating the certainty of his election as a representative to the Massachusetts General Court, the state legislature. The ballots handdelivered to voters will make certain of that. Something must be done to mark the occasion. Club members call to the bartender, Tom Hussion. A special drink for their man!

Hussion pulls out a bottle of fine whiskey, maybe rye, maybe bourbon. He quickly cuts a lemon, squeezing the juice into the glass. In goes sugar to create a traditional whiskey sour. But this is not enough for the occasion. Hussion adds a squeeze from an orange and then a dash of grenadine, which turns the libation a pleasing rose color. He stirs the drink thoroughly and hands it to the man who had demanded the tribute. The man sips, grins, and raises his glass; "This is *excellent*. I stand drinks for all!" Hussion mixes and pours as the crowd toasts Lomasney. They drink, they cheer, and they drink some more. Hussion hurries to keep the glasses filled.

"Sir, what do you name this?" one wag calls out, raising his glass unsteadily.

The man who requested the drink has a ready answer. "We'll call it the Ward Eight," he says. The crowd roars its approval.

The drink would become a staple at Locke-Ober, linking the restaurant to the story of the Mahatma. Its popularity spread through the city and then through the region, becoming by 1920, "The Famous Ward Eight."

An ironic postscript finishes the myth. Lomasney was a teetotaler and possibly a supporter of Prohibition, which would officially drain the city dry of liquor. Thus, Boston's most famous cocktail was linked to one of its driest politicians.

And that's the story of Boston's Ward Eight, repeated frequently in newspapers, magazines, and books and spread by the Internet.

But is it the real story?

Dig a bit, and you find there are holes the size of the old Boston Garden in the generally accepted story of the Ward Eight. First, let's take the recipe. Grenadine wouldn't be popular until the 1910s, and it would have been unusual to create a drink with the red syrup made from sugar and pomegranates in 1898. There are recipes for the Ward Eight in drinking manuals of the 1920s through 1940s, but the ingredients, proportions, and garnishes are inconsistent. That date of 1898 is also odd. Lomasney would win many elections, and there's no clear reason why that date stands out as a particular electoral success. His handpicked candidates would actually suffer a defeat that election season.

We will dissect some of the mysteries of the Ward Eight. But first let's make the real point: It doesn't matter.

It's not that truth is unimportant. It's that, in this case, it's irrelevant.

The story of the Ward Eight has become so ingrained in Boston's history that the truth—like actual voting totals in Mayor Curley's Boston—is beside the point. The parts are greater than the sum. The Ward Eight legend reflects the various aspects that help create the particular quality of Boston's drinking history.

In fact, it's a little like this book. This is a history of drinking in Boston; a slightly idiosyncratic project inspired by the newly awakened interest in cocktails, in speakeasy culture, and in the glamour of Rat-Pack style nightclubs and classic cocktail lounges. Certainly, Boston has been maligned for its Puritan rigidity and its Brahmin reticence; the words "Banned in" flow naturally to the kicker "Boston." And yet the city and its pioneering bartenders have been among those at the forefront of a new cocktail culture, fueled by a geekish interest in old drinks with fresh ingredients. But, as it turns out, Boston has a long drinking history, with patterns that began with the city's founding and continued through its Revolutionary period and into the nineteenth century.

This book explores the unique threads that weave through Boston's drinking history, in particular, the push and pull between the Puritan ethic of control and social approbation and a revolutionary spirit of personal expression and brazen townie pride. The temperance movement was nurtured by New England reformers and yet so was the Americanized vision of the Irish pub. This is a history of the saloons of the late eighteenth and early nineteenth century when immigrants—Irish, Italian, Jewish—added their blend to the melting pot of American culture on Boston streets. This book peeks inside the 1920s speakeasies and the glamorous nightclubs of the 1940s and 1950s; it catches a riff of music from the hot spots of jazz and blues and a waft of cigarette smoke from the corner tavern in Dorchester and Southie; it meanders through the city's bars and watering holes, its speakeasies and nightclubs. Of course, this literary pub crawl can't hit every spot or tell every story; closing time and book deadlines are something you can't argue with. It's a taste and a sip, an exercise in moderation.

There are already many books on alcohol, ranging from sober histories of American drinking patterns to treatises on the health impacts of overindulgence. There are guidebooks to Boston's bar scene,

Courtesy of the Trustees of the Boston Public Library.

today and yesterday, from delightful to dive. Cocktail recipe books are appearing as fast as beer orders after a Red Sox win.

This book is something different.

What you hold in your hands is a historical cocktail. A bit of this. A lot of that. But all within the context of the spirit of the city on the Charles. This is a book about drinking in Boston. Not New York. Not Chicago. Not the nation. While most of the history books cited above mention Boston, few of them dwell on the Hub, with the exception of the Colonial and Revolutionary period.

For example, most histories of Prohibition sidestep Boston as if, somehow, the City on the Hill never felt the touch of the temperance movement or the chill of the Volstead Act. Chicago's gang wars and mob mastermind Al Capone are known to all, and Hollywood has enshrined the speakeasies of New York and Los Angeles, where a password granted admittance into glamorous caverns of flappers, hip flasks, and martini glasses. Documentaries and books about the temperance movement that led to passage of the Eighteenth Amendment highlight the antics of a toad-faced, hatchet-wielding Carrie Nation as she busted up Kansas bars in her one-woman crusade against Demon Rum. Even to many Bostonians, Prohibition only conjures tales of Joseph Kennedy, Sr., and his mythical bootlegging, as if the Kennedy patriarch alone could have been responsible for the booze that fueled the city from 1920 to 1933.

Yet all the upheavals and hypocrisies, the battle between Wets and Drys, and the hide-and-seek of rum-runners, peepholes, and police— all this happened in Boston and left an indelible impact on the city's drinking life. The temperance movement, often interpreted today as a kind of proto-feminist crusade by suffragettes in long frocks, had roots among Boston's male Brahmin bluebloods, the intellectual builders of

18

"the Athens of America." They added a peculiarly New England twist to the Dry crusade cocktail by focusing on the negative health effects of alcohol, rather than its inherent evil. Boston even had its own Capone, an enigmatic bootlegger and racketeer who was spoken about in whispers until he was gunned down in a hail of bullets.

Thus, a large part of the history of Boston's drinking is what happened when the town went dry.

So we have carefully chosen our recipe. We throw in a gill of spirits from the Revolutionary period, a jigger from the saloon era, bitters from Prohibition, and a cherry from the nightclub experience. We garnish with the emergence of a new interest in cocktails. We will chase it with a good slug of neighborhood attitude, the craft of the corner bar. We will drink with relish and moderation, aware that the setting of where we drink and how we are treated there is as important as what we drink. Bartender John Gertsen from the bar Drink in the Fort Point neighborhood of Boston, explains this by citing this slogan: "Bartenders don't serve drinks. Bartenders serve people."

This is what Boston has become known for. The place where everybody knows your name. Nearly twenty years after Norm and Cliff sipped their last beers in the long-running TV series "Cheers," tourists still line up outside the former Bull & Finch Pub on Beacon Street, which supplied the exterior shots for the show. Bar culture isn't unique to Boston, but Boston seems to epitomize the mythology of the home away from home, the "great good place," to borrow a term from writer Ray Oldenburg, where people gather for public socializing.

From April 2006 to July 2011, writer Lauren Clark explored Boston's imbibing culture in her influential blog, *Drink Boston*. Clark suspended the blog when she moved from Boston, but she still has strong and warm feelings about the Hub. Clark was pressed by this author on why she originally chose to write about Boston's drinking. She pondered for a few seconds: "Boston was and is a singular town when it comes to drinking," she says. "We've got the history. We have a population that likes to drink. We've got the smart, creative intelligent types who like craft beer, good wine, and good cocktails. We also have the 'Hey, we work hard–let's go out and get shitfaced.' All those things combined just make Boston a town I want to embrace for its drinking."

Boston is, indeed, a singular place for drinking. Like the Ward Eight, the drinking history comes loaded with lore, both sweet and bitter, gaudy and guarded, and packs a punch, whether shaken or stirred.

Take a last sip of the drink. Put down the empty glass. We have a lot to cover. And if you want real answers about the mystery of the Ward Eight, you'll have to read on.

Mayor Curley accepts a case of Budweiser shortly after Repeal.
Courtesy of the Trustees of the Boston Public Library.

WARD EIGHT

(One possible version.)

2 ounces rye whiskey *(No rye? Use bourbon.)*
¾ ounce fresh-squeezed lemon juice
½ ounce real pomegranate grenadine

Shake all ingredients very well over ice
and strain into a chilled cocktail glass.

Garnish with orange wheel and
cherry if desired.

Tremont Street from Court to Bromfield St.
As it appeared in 1800.

kiel Price. Rufus G. Amory.　　Cemetary.　　King's Chapel.　School St.

View of Tremont Street from Bromfield to West Street.
As it appeared in 1800.

House and Garden of
John Andrews Esq.　　Winter St. Thos Thompson. Mr. Cole. Mr. Ballard.

View of Tremont Street from West Street to Boylston Street,
As it appeared in 1800.

Scales.　　　　　Mason St. Tavern (Mr. Hatch)　　　　Haymarket

View of Boylston St. from Tremont to Carver.
As it appeared in 1800.

J. T. Apthorp.　　James Phillips　Tan Yard.　Jos. Allen.　David Townsend's House & Inspection Office

TAVERNS IN OLD BOSTON:
THE SPIRIT
OF REVOLUTION

The days are short, the weather's cold,
By tavern fires tales are told.
Some ask for dram when first come in,
Others with flip and bounce begin.

—*New England Almanac,* circa 1702

The place would have been dark by modern standards and smoky from candles and a crackling fire or hazy from the puffing of clay pipes. A patron might look in vain for a chair—these were prized commodities in taverns and were often few in number. He might have to press his backside against that of another man to share a seat, near the buffet where food and drink were served. Whereas in a church he might have to look for the section reserved for his particular social class, here, in the tavern, he might mingle with men of all sorts—farmers, sailors, saddle makers, blacksmiths, even a judge. He might ask for ale or beer or hard cider or a "bounce," a kind of mixed drink, or a flip—a mug of beer with rum, molasses, and sugar stirred with a hot poker until it foamed and bubbled. His host might pour him something from the nearby barrels of rum, cider, and beer, tossing in sugar or spice from the jars around him. The patron would drink from a pewter pot or flagon or even a leather cup, more rarely a glass vessel. The drink would not be expensive—the price of liquor was strictly regulated in Colonial Boston, as was the licensing of ordinaries (or inns) and taverns.

The patron would trade news and stories with other patrons, learning the latest news from other parts of the Commonwealth or even England. He might be served by a woman; widows often took over the businesses of taverns from deceased husbands. In a few sips, he would feel the warm glow that alcohol gives; he might—were he religious—begin to feel a tinge of apprehension or guilt. Perhaps he was not among the chosen that his Puritan minister insisted would get to heaven. Then again, the Reverend Increase Mather himself had called drink "a good creature of God," even though the minister also warned against spirits-induced debauchery.

It would be hard not to feel good in the tavern, lively with conversation and the bidding of good cheer and the candlelight, so much brighter than his one-room home and its single wick. Here a friend might stand him to a drink; another man might insist that all drink to the health of the king although some will mutter darkly about the onerous demands of the Crown. The patron might ask for a last mug and heave a sigh of contentment.

Such might have been the experience of a Bostonian walking into a local tavern circa 1740.

That Boston has always been a drinking man's (and sometimes woman's) town is revealed in the stories of its early taverns, places with evocative, jolly-old-England names like the Green Dragon, Bunch of Grapes,

King's Arms, Cromwell's Head, Castle Tavern, Royal Exchange, Ship Tavern, Red Lion, Salutation, and Blue Anchor. It's no surprise then that Boston, like many towns in the Colonial period had popular taverns and inns. It's also not surprising that most of these places have long vanished, given Boston's record of demolition and renewal (consider the way Boston's West End and raffish Scollay Square were swept away in the 1960s). A bit more surprising is how their memory has been lovingly—if over-romantically—preserved in numerous historical treatises of the nineteenth and early twentieth century by local historians seeking to celebrate "old Boston." Even those blue-blood historians who decried the excesses of the nineteenth-century saloon recognized the taverns' pivotal roles in the development of Colonial society and, in particular, the emergence of social agitation that eventually ejected British rule.

Taverns, writes W. J. Rorabaugh in *The Alcoholic Republic*, "were certainly seed beds of the Revolution, the places where British tyranny was condemned, militiamen organized, and independence plotted." Likewise, David W. Conroy, author of *In Public Houses: Drink and the Revolution of Authority in Colonial Massachusetts*, contends that taverns were "a public stage upon which men, and sometimes women, spoke and acted in ways that sometimes tested—and ultimately challenged—the authority of their rulers and social superiors in the hierarchy of Massachusetts society."

The regulation of early taverns also revealed a basic tension that runs through any history of Boston's relationship with alcohol—the push-pull between personal liberty and public dictums, between telling people what they should do for their own good and letting them define goodness in their own personal way.

What is also clear is this: The early inhabitants of Boston loved their booze. Take those much-maligned Puritans, who helped build what they envisioned as a City upon a Hill. They, too, drank with great gusto even as they railed against drunkenness and sought to restrict the commercialization of drinking. Alcohol historians say the United States has always been one of the world's great drinking countries. Before the 1750s nearly all Americans of all ranks drank heavily, sometimes to the point of intoxication. The price of liquor at inns was highly regulated, which kept it affordable for travelers as well as residents. In the mid-1630s, the

Royal Exchange Tavern near what is now the Old State House.
Courtesy of the Trustees of the Boston Public Library.

legal charge for a quart of ale or a quart of beer at an inn was a penny; the price of a meal was sixpence. As Boston's population grew, so did the number of taverns, from 27 licensees in 1677 to 134 in 1765, according to tavern historian Gavin R. Nathan. The early taverns sold mostly beer and ale; some also sold wine. Gradually taste grew for harder stuff; the annual per capita consumption of hard liquor, mostly rum, reached 3.7 gallons in the Colonial period.

Another social need drove the growth of drinking establishments. Most of the taverns functioned as inns, or "ordinaries" as they were called, catering to the business travel of a burgeoning capitalist economy. Eight years after the town was established in 1630, Boston had two ordinaries, where a stranger could find a meal and a bed. Hospitality soon became a business that was regulated, along with the price of labor and food and just about everything else. For a set fee a traveler could get a meal, a drink, and a bed, even if travelers often had to share the bed. By 1647, the number of applicants for licenses to keep taverns had increased so much that the Massachusetts General Court passed on the licensing authority to local communities. These early taverns were, however, not operated for the convenience of travelers as much as for the pleasure of neighbors who wanted a place to gather; they quickly became community fixtures.

Even as taverns were eagerly welcomed, they were criticized. In 1675, the Reverend Cotton Mather, son of Increase Mather, complained that every other house in Boston was a tavern, a complaint that would be repeated through the next century. The oft-dour John Adams groused in his diary that inns and taverns were numerous in the province, but not numerous enough to handle the number of travelers and, besides, the accommodations were miserable. "Yet, if you sit the evening, you will find the house full of people drinking drams, flip, toddy, carousing, swearing; but especially plotting with the landlord to get him at the next town meeting, an election either for selectman or representative." Such complaints could not stem the popularity of the lure of drinks with friends by a crackling fire. Tavern historian Edward Field quotes an unnamed writer as declaring: "The New Englanders all want to be politicians and therefore love the taverns and grog-bowl over which they do their business and drink from morning till night." Even if the customers were primarily men, women numbered among tavern owners; in 1714 of thirty-four inn holders, twelve were women and of forty-two retailers of liquor, seventeen were female.

New Englanders particularly favored cider, which was cheap and plentiful and easily produced from apples. Tavern historian Alice Morse Earle describes it thus:

> *All the colonists drank cider, old and young and in all places,—funerals, weddings, ordaining, vestry-meetings, church raisings, etc. Infants in arms drank mulled hard cider at night, a beverage which would kill a modern babe. It was supplied to students at Harvard and Yale colleges at dinner and bever, being passed in two-quart tankards from hand to hand down the commons table. Old men began the day with a quart or more of hard cider before breakfast. Delicate women drank hard cider. All laborers in the field drank it in great draughts that were often liberally fortified with drams of New England rum.*

Mrs. Earle, a writer long on anecdotes and short on sources, may have been exaggerating, but given the questionable water supplies, many Colonists believed that drinking some form of liquor was safer than drinking water. Cider was just one option. Colonial Bostonians also drank punch, grog, Madeira, sherry toddy, claret, sangaree, brandy, "Jonava" or gin, metheglin (or spiced mead), home-brewed beer, and ale. They drank beer brewed from spruce, birch, and sassafras bark or with herbs and pumpkin and apple paring, with added molasses, maple syrup, and beet tops. Punch was extremely popular, and every family who could afford one had a punch bowl. Whether the punch inside was strong is another matter. In 1785, eighty people attending a minister's ordination managed to put away thirty bowls of punch before the service. At the dinner afterwards, sixty-eight guests consumed "forty-four bowls of punch, eighteen bottles of wine, eight bowls of brandy, and a quantity of cherry rum," Earle writes, neglecting to add, "*Hic.*"

Flip was another popular pick-me-up. Rum, sugar, and molasses—or sometimes cream and eggs—were added to a mug of beer. A poker or finger-thick metal stick was heated up and thrust into the mug to make the mixture foam and bubble and give it a particularly prized bitter taste. The alcohol would take care of any bacteria in the eggs (indeed, eggs would become popular additions to a variety of drinks) and the blend of flavors and heat made it a popular drink in the days before central heating. The ever-game Mrs. Earle decided she would try this as part of the research for her book: "Alas, I had neither the tastes nor the digestion of my Revolutionary sires and the indescribable scorched and puckering bitterness of taste and pungency of smell of that rank compound which was flip will serve for some time in my memory as an antidote from any overweening longing for the good old times."

Starting about the mid-1700s, the growing popularity of rum, a more potent brew made from sugar cane, became a cause for public concern. The advent of the rum trade began to stiffen resistance to drinking, something never far below the surface of strict Colonial life. In 1657, the General Court of Massachusetts jumped in to try to restrict the sale of strong spirits. Yet by the next year, Increase Mather was lamenting, "They that are poor and wicked, too, can for a penny make themselves drunk." An influential pamphlet, "Serious address to those who unnecessarily frequent the tavern, and often spend the evening in publick houses," published in 1726, sounded an alarm that would echo through the decades until it reached an apotheosis in 1919:

> *For as we fear, taverns are multiplied among us beyond the bounds of real necessity and even to a fault, if not a scandal, so likewise that too many of them prove nurseries of vice being prostituted by multitudes to an ill use even the serving of diverse lusts and pleasures which war against the soul or at best the wasting away of many precious hours in unprofitable amusements...*

The abuse of alcohol and the ravages of addiction, both then and now, should not be minimized even if the warnings of eighteenth-century preachers seem quaint. However, the admonishment against "wasting away of many precious hours" in taverns was overzealous prudery. Taverns were one of the few places in Colonial Massachusetts where a person could unwind, not only from the stresses of this life but also from thoughts of the next. As Conroy drily explains it: "Worshipping a Calvinist God could be an intimidating experience. One was never sure of salvation." Taverns also tended to level the social playing field; patrons were not segregated as they were in church, according to family or social hierarchy, instead they mingled and rubbed elbows with people from various walks of life. It should be added, though, that different communities—then, as today—did self-select among different taverns. According to historian Samuel Adams Drake, the more wealthy, Royalist supporters tended to frequent the British Coffee-House, an inn and drinking establishment on the north side of what is now State Street, while the more radical-minded drank at the Bunch of Grapes located near the waterfront. Even when the patrons were from varied social classes, more prominent members of society were treated deferentially. Judge Samuel Sewall, of whom more will be said, felt no fear of being called into a tavern of rowdy men, ordering them to calm down and, even more amazingly, having them each write down their names so more punishment could be doled out later.

With the liberating warmth of spirits, citizens were more likely to freely express opinions. "Here, men interacted with each other on a common level, citizens all," Conroy notes. After patiently listening to sermons in unheated churches, or attending meetings in the cold expanse of the Boston Town House, a large structure used as a seat of government and as a commercial space, citizens would crowd into the warm comfort of taverns, which were built nearby by design, a practice sanctioned by authorities. Moreover, taverns were often used for official meetings and legal proceedings. Thus local drinking establishments were woven into the very social fabric of New England and were arguably the most numerous public institutions of the Colonial period. Patrons were expected to be convivial, friendly, and talkative, but remain sober, more or less. A tall order as more potent alcohol became increasingly available. Even as reformers sought to limit the consumption of rum, more places began to serve this libation that would play such a major role in the triangular trade of slave, sugar, and rum.

Perhaps one of the more intriguing aspects of early taverns is their role as a setting for legal proceedings. Documentation of this practice is contained in the diary of Judge Samuel Sewall, an interesting if problematic figure in New England history. Born in England in 1652, Sewall came to Newbury, north of Boston, in 1661 as a young boy. He studied at Harvard, married, worked as a merchant, and was elected in 1684 to the Commonwealth's General Court. In 1692, he was appointed as one of the nine judges on the notorious witchcraft trials in Salem and was among those watching as nineteen men and women were executed on witchcraft charges, perhaps one of the most horrific miscarriages of justice in Colonial America. In a remarkable turnaround, Sewall—alone of the witchcraft judges—was overcome with guilt over his role and repented in a public address on January 14, 1697. He went on to live a long and productive life (unlike the witchcraft trial victims) as a Superior Court judge and theologian. He married three times, raised numerous children and grandchildren, and died in 1730 at age seventy-seven.

Sewall also kept a meticulous diary for fifty-seven years in which he recorded the minutia of his life—details that though they may have seemed trivial at the time have over the years been vital to our understanding the social history of the Colonial period. From his diary, we know that court sessions were sometimes held in nearby taverns; indeed sessions that ended in the Town House sometimes resumed in a nearby tavern. A frequently used spot for court was the Blue Anchor Tavern (sometimes referred to as the Blew Anchor), run by George Monk (sometimes spelled Monck), which stood on the east side of Washington Street between State and Water streets. The court also met in a tavern run by John Turner, and Sewall once waited on the court at the Green Dragon to testify. When the Boston Town House burned in 1747, sessions were held at the Royal Exchange Tavern nearby.

Although it's not entirely clear if drinking occurred during legal proceedings, one wonders if it would have inspired more leniency for insubordinates? Or did it steel judges for harsh decisions? Consider Sewall's entry for 1699: "Joseph Indian is acquitted. James Morgan is sent to, and acquainted that he must dye next Thorsday (sic), and ordered that Mr. Mather be acquainted with it who is to preach the Lecture....Mr. Stoughton and Dudley voted not in the Judgment, and went off the Bench when Sentence was to be passed. Major Richards slid off too. Judgment was voted at George Monk's [the Blue Anchor Tavern] before rose from Table, on Thorsday (sic)."

James Morgan was indeed later executed.

The early Boston tavern (according to a *Boston Globe* article tellingly written during the height of Prohibition in 1922) was "a social center of eminent respectability, patronized by the leading citizens. And the tavern keeper, accordingly, was a man of prominence and substance." Monk himself cut a colorful figure. In 1686, London bookseller and author John Dunton described Monk in glowing terms: "a person so remarkable that, had I not been acquainted with him, it would be a hard matter to make any New England man believe that I had been in Boston. There was no house in Boston more noted than George Monk's or where a man might meet with better entertainment. He was so much the life and spirit of the Guests that came to his house that it was almost impossible not to be cheerful in his company." Incidentally, Monk profited from his tavern turning courtroom. On one occasion when the General Court sat in on an election banquet, circa 1658, the wine bill for 204 diners ran up to 72 bottles of Madeira, 28 of Lisbon, 17 of port, 10 of claret, 15 of porter, and 50 double-bowls of punch, besides cider.

Whether Sewall was an enforcer or participant, the Blue Anchor played a special role in his life, not only as a place where he heard cases, but as a spot where he dined and socialized. That he, like so many others, found some comfort in a tavern hardly detracts from his legacy. Take this diary notation, "Went to George Monk's and paid him in full, drank half a pint of Wine together." In those few words, the learned judge paints a portrait of a place where he and a tavern keeper can meet and drink together on more or less equal footing and in equal comfort.

That we know about many of these early taverns is largely due to the efforts of historian Samuel Adams Drake, a Civil War veteran, a newspaper man, a reporter for the Associated Press, and the author of numerous books on New England history. In 1886, he published the first edition of his popular book, *Old Boston Taverns and Tavern Clubs* (reprinted in 1917), which was cited frequently (with and without attribution) by many historians who followed. Alice Morse Earle, the author of *Stagecoach and Tavern Days*, seemed to base much of her research on Drake's work, and Arthur Brayley, known for his history of the Boston Fire Department, shamelessly lifts Drake's material wholesale for a lengthy five-part series on "Boston's Famous Colonial Taverns" that ran in the *Boston Globe* in August 1900.

Drake concluded that Boston's first licensed ordinary, an inn run by Samuel Cole, dates back to 1634 and was located near what is Washington Street in the Downtown Crossing section of Boston today. (The establishment was later called the Ship Tavern; it was destroyed in a huge fire in 1711.) Other taverns followed: King's Arms in what is now Dock Square, the Golden Ball Tavern on Merchants Row, the Castle Tavern, also in Dock Square, and the Royal Exchange on what is now State Street. The Sign of the Lamb Tavern was established by 1746, and in 1767 it was the headquarters for the first stagecoach line to run between Boston and Providence. The Exchange became a popular spot, and Sewall mentions it a number of times in his diary. The Exchange is also part of the backdrop of Paul Revere's print of the Boston Massacre of 1770, when British soldiers fired upon a patriot mob that had been harassing them. At that time the tavern was popular among British soldiers who were then being stationed in Boston. When the smoke cleared, the body of the first victim, Crispus Attucks (who was also identified as

Michael Johnson), was carried into the Exchange. The next day, Dr. Benjamin Church performed the autopsy there, this being a time when the town had neither a hospital nor a mortuary.

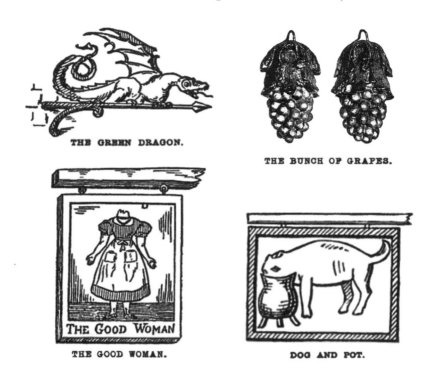

THE GREEN DRAGON.

THE BUNCH OF GRAPES.

THE GOOD WOMAN.

DOG AND POT.

Illustrations of Colonial tavern signs featuring the Green Dragon, Bunch of Grapes, the Good Woman, and Dog and Pot from Old Boston Taverns and Tavern Clubs *by Samuel Adams Drake.*

In the North End, on what is now Richmond Street, a Quaker named Nicholas Upshall ran the Red Lion. According to Drake, Upshall was jailed by Puritan authorities for his "outspoken condemnation." Nearby on North Street, the Salutation served shipwrights; caulkers; carpenters who made ship spars, masts, and booms; and others working in the nearby shipyards and was the site for Whig meetings by politicians seeking to court support. Drake concludes that the word "caucus" was derived from the spirited meetings of caulkers and others in these establishments. The inn's sign showed two citizens with their hands extended and thus neighbors called the place "The Two Palaverers." The British Coffee-House on King Street became the American Coffee-House on State Street. Here Revolutionary-era patriot and lawyer James Otis, who had argued passionately against British oppression, got into a brawl with Royalist supporters and was badly beaten. His later fits of insanity were attributed to his head wound, and he was killed by a bolt of lightning in 1783. Cromwell's Head on School Street displayed a sign in the grim likeness of Oliver Cromwell, the Lord Protector who overthrew the British monarchy in 1649 and temporarily established a republic. (After his death by natural causes, Cromwell's body was reportedly dug up, its head cut off and displayed on a pole outside Westminster Abbey. Tavern owner Joshua Brackett apparently had a heightened appetite for the macabre.)

The Bunch of Grapes tavern—and a replica of a bunch of the aforementioned fruit hung outside—was located on Kilby and what is now State Street. It may have opened as early as 1680, but the building was destroyed in the 1711 blaze and rebuilt in 1712. "From that time, until after the Revolution, it appears to have always been open as a public inn, and as such, is feelingly referred to by one old traveler as the best punch-house to be found in all Boston," Drake writes. After the Revolution, General George Washington was feted there and "joy and gratitude sat on every countenance and smiled in every eye," according to a contemporary newspaper account. In 1780, the French General Lafayette was received there when he brought word that France would support the patriots.

Drake even imagines what a feast would be like in the Bunch of Grapes during the Revolutionary period: At 2 pm the bell would ring for dinner, and guests were served salmon, veal, beef, mutton, fowl, ham, vegetables, and pudding, each one with his pint of Madeira set before him. The tavern served as the first meeting place (from 1733) of the Grand Lodge of Masons in Massachusetts and of its first chartered lodge, St. John's Lodge.

Perhaps best known of the many early taverns was the Green Dragon, which stood on what is now Union Street. From the front of the building jutted a distinctive thick copper plate of a monstrous reptile with a curled tail and a fearful tongue, "the wonder of all the boys who dwelt in the neighborhood," writes historian James Shurtleff. Built in 1680 and demolished in 1828, "it became as famous as any private edifice—if such it could be called, considering the public uses to which it was frequently put—that could be found upon the peninsula." In 1764, after passing through various owners, it was purchased by members of the St. Andrew's Lodge of Freemasons. The three-story building had common rooms on its first floor, a large hall for public and Masonic meetings on its second, and sleeping apartments in its attic. It was on the first floor that a secret society met and hatched plots that would launch a new nation.

In the fall of 1774 and winter of 1775, discontent was brewing in Boston over the governance of the British, who were increasingly seen by a certain portion of the population as brutal taskmasters. The dissenters, who would later be called patriots, included Samuel Adams (cousin to John Adams), Paul Revere, John Hancock, James Otis, Dr. Joseph Warren, and Dr. Benjamin Church. Their group underwent various transformations, eventually becoming the Sons of Liberty. They would meet at the Green Dragon to compare information they had gathered about the movements of British soldiers. The committee was astonished to find that their activities were almost always immediately known to

General Thomas Gage, the British commander, even though all the men were sworn to secrecy. That the men believed that something said in a bar would actually be kept secret was amazing. And, indeed, it was one of the men—Dr. Church—who was found to be betraying his comrades by sending secret communications to the British. The men had reason to feel safe in the Green Dragon; the tavern had already played a key role in the road to revolution. After a huge meeting in November 1773 at the Old South Meeting House (the former church still stands on Washington Street) in which citizens railed against British imposition of a tea tax, the Sons of Liberty were determined

The new Green Dragon on Marshall Street.

to take further action. On December 15, they gathered at the Green Dragon and hatched a plot. The next night, dressed as Indians, the Sons crept up to the three ships where the tea was held, dashed on board, and tossed tea crates overboard. The Boston Tea Party was a pivotal act in the American Revolution and the reference point for any number of political movements that have followed. While a few have made the argument that the Tea Party was planned in the Hancock Tavern or even the Salutation Tavern, evidence suggests that the Green Dragon was the staging ground. As Drake writes, "It represented the muscle of the Revolution."

The freedom experienced in the Colonial tavern, Conroy argues, led to the desire for freedom in other aspects of life. Many tavern owners played an active role in opposing the status quo. Of the 355 Sons of Liberty identified in 1769, about 26 had liquor retail or tavern licenses, and Conroy has found close connections were forged among the liquor men and the civil and militia officers through the Sons' activities. "Selectmen and drink sellers worked together in the organization of protest," he writes. In 1768, the Sons commissioned an elaborate silver punch bowl from Paul Revere; rum was a common ingredient in the punch of that day. Revere may be best known for his famous ride, but he was a far more skillful artist than horseman. His punch bowl is, however, a masterpiece of elegance. Inscribed with the names of fifteen associates of the Sons, it was created as a symbol of how all gathered to drink together in equality. The gleaming punch bowl is now in the possession of the Museum of Fine Arts in Boston.

The success of the Revolution increased the prestige of the taverns. It's doubtful that genteel writers like Drake or proper Bostonians such as Mrs. Earle would otherwise have dipped quill in pot to write about these establishments had it not been for their important role in that history. In fact, Drake envisions his history of taverns as a kind of dirge or lament. "There are certainly no longer any taverns in New England," is his mournful opening statement. "Not a single specimen of the old-time hostelries now remains in Boston. All is changed. The demon demolition is everywhere."

But reverence for Revolutionary taverns did not extend to the saloons of the late nineteenth and early twentieth century, increasingly perceived by elites as dens for drinking and debauchery. Boston town, too, was changing. The narrow streets were too confining and were widened. The growing population needed more room: the Back Bay was filled in to create a new neighborhood, the harbor line pushed outward. The Green Dragon was demolished to widen Green Dragon Lane, renamed Union Street, and the famous sign has disappeared. A plaque was placed on its approximate location in 1892; it was removed in 1960 and turned over to The Bostonian Society. Two bunches of the wooden grapes used as the sign for the Bunch of Grapes have been lovingly preserved by St. John's Lodge even as the tavern and others like it disappeared.

The "tavern" of Drake's romantic vision may have been gone, but the era of the saloon and the pub was just beginning—as well as the stirrings that would lead to Prohibition. "No words need be wasted upon the present degradation which the name of tavern implies to polite ears. In most minds it is now associated with the slums of the city," Drake writes, foreshadowing the future. "Old Boston" was giving way to a new kind of urban society with different thirsts, tastes, and habits.

FISH HOUSE PUNCH

(From Jerry Thomas's How to Mix Drinks, *1862.*
Said to be a favorite of John Adams.)

⅓ pint lemon juice
¾ pound white sugar
1 pint of mixture (see below)
2 ½ pints cold water
The above is generally sufficient for one person.

The mixture: ¼ pint of peach brandy, ½ pint of
Cognac, and ¼ pint of Jamaica rum.

Stir ingredients together in a large pot
and when ready, pour over ice.

McGreevy's Third Base Saloon.
Courtesy of the Trustees of the Boston Public Library.

BOSTON'S SALOON HISTORY: DEMOCRACY ON TAP

The tavern will compare favorably with the church. The church is the place where prayers and sermons are delivered, but the tavern is where they are to take effect and if the former are good, the latter cannot be bad.

—Henry David Thoreau, circa 1865

The saloon is the most democratic of institutions.

—Raymond Calkins, *Substitutes for the Saloon*

This was not a bar. It was a shrine, a temple dedicated to all things baseball, in the old days before million-dollar contracts, the designated hitter, and steroid testing. The walls were plastered with photos and souvenirs that would make the boy inside the man tremble with awe. Faces from the hometown teams, the Boston Braves and the Boston Americans (who would become the Red Sox), gazed out from their frames, frozen in black-and-white glory. A clock with a baseball bat for a pendulum and weighted with a baseball marked the time between games. The room was lit from frosted light fixtures in the shapes of baseballs attached to bats hung from the ceiling. These were no ordinary bats, however; they had once been swung by the likes of Cy Young and Freddy Parent and other demigods in the pantheon of America's favorite pastime. A gold medal once given to former Boston Beaneater player Michael "King" Kelly by the *Boston Globe* in October 1887 was hung in a place of honor. All this wonder was best appreciated with a drink in hand. An ornately carved bar stretched the length of the room, and behind it were taps for beer and bottles neatly stacked on shelves amid more memorabilia. Conversation and laughter were punctuated by orders: "One beer." "A Bronx." "Musty." "Gin fizz." Patrons would break into song, perhaps "Sweet Adeline" or, more likely, "Tessie." This Broadway tune had become the song of the Royal Rooters, the fervent fan club of the Red Sox, who now reigned over a new gem of a ballpark in the Fenway. If an argument broke out or a discussion got too heated—Who was the best outfielder? Duffy Lewis, Tris Speaker, or Harry Hooper? How did that new pitcher named Babe compare to Smoky Joe Wood??—the bar owner would break in with his answer. He was a powerfully built but short fellow with apple cheeks and a handlebar mustache as lush as the Public Garden in spring. He was as nice a fellow as you would be likely to meet, but he had the quiet authority of a fan so knowledgeable and devoted that he had become legend around the country. "Enough said!" Michael T. McGreevy[1] would roar, and the arguing patrons would quiet, sometimes grumpily, sometimes with a rueful grin. "Nuf Ced" McGreevy's word was law.

---

[1] There are huge disagreements on the correct spelling of Michael T. McGreevy's last name. Newspapers of the era spell it both McGreevy and McGreevey; the collection of his donated photos to the Boston Public Library is called the "McGreevey Collection." However, two signatures in that collection spell the name McGreevy. Likewise, Nuf Ced is often rendered as Nuff-Ced, Nuff Sed, or other variations.

This was the bar called Third Base, that is to say, the last stop before home, and McGreevy's tavern certainly was a home away from home for many Bostonians. This is where players and fans, enterprising businessmen and sweaty workmen all sipped their beers and gin fizzes and talked sports, blissfully unaware that two dry spells loomed on the horizon. One would last thirteen years and bring to a close the culture of the nineteenth-century Boston barroom. The other would last eighty-six years, leaving heartbreak and frustration in its wake. Who can say which was worse?

As the eighteenth century rolled into the nineteenth century, Boston's drinking customs and habits were shifting along with its skyline. The revered taverns of the Colonial period, with their conviviality and hospitality, were disappearing amid the relentless development of a growing city. Grander hotels and finer restaurants began to dot the downtown along with saloons, barrooms, and unapologetic dives. Grog was being replaced by more sophisticated concoctions that better utilized the omnipresent and resilient liquor of choice, rum. Behind the bar, Bostonians were inventive with their spirits. Charles Dickens, who visited the city in 1842, described how a hotel bar initiated him "into the mysteries of the Gin-sling, Cocktail, Sangaree, Mint Julep, Sherry-cobbler, Timber Doodle, and other rare drinks." (The Timber Doodle was so rare that its recipe remains unknown today.) In 1862, a British mixing manual singled out a Columbia Skin as a "Boston drink, and is made the same as a whiskey skin," that is, with a wine glass of Scotch whiskey, a piece of lemon peel, and a tumbler half filled with boiling water.

Whether patrons were sipping sherry cobblers in a bar of a grand hotel or quaffing ale in a corner tavern, Boston's drinking establishments were, on the whole, welcoming places where men—and it was mostly men—drank together. Nathaniel Hawthorne, author of *The Scarlet Letter*, would often travel into Boston for a meal and a drink, including a visit to Parker's, a grog shop of the 1850s, at 4 Court Square. He writes:

> *At the counter stand, at almost all hours,—certainly at all hours when I have chanced to observe,—tipplers, either taking a solitary glass or treating all round, veteran topers, flashy young men, visitors from the country, the various petty officers connected with the law, whom the vicinity of the Court House brings hither. Chiefly, they drink plain liquors, gin, brandy or whiskey, sometimes a Tom and Jerry, a gin cocktail (which the bartender makes artistically, tossing it in a large parabola from one tumbler to another until fit for drinking), a brandy smash, and numerous other concoctions. All this toping goes forward with little or no apparent exhilaration of spirits; nor does this seem to be the object sought,—it being rather, I imagine, to create a titillation of the coats of the stomach, and a general sense of invigoration, without affecting the brain. Very seldom does a man grow wild and unruly.*

Drunkenness was not the aim—drinking together was. Yet despite Hawthorne's observation that only a few patrons would discretely and quietly get soused, other proper Bostonians were alarmed at the incidents of excessive public drinking. Americans, in general, began to drink more and harder spirits in the latter part of the nineteenth century. "Although [Americans were] never a notably sober people, their drinking developed during the period to become a national menace," said Otto Bettman in *The Good Old Days: They Were Terrible!* Per capita yearly consumption of alcohol increased from eight gallons in 1878 to seventeen gallons in 1898. It was common to stand friends, or an entire crowd, to a round of drinks. The custom of sipping small daily doses or drams as a perceived health benefit had given way to sustained consumption, with round after round of toasting this one's and that one's health, until all were reeling and slurring and looking rather worse for the wear. Drinking together, even to excess, symbolized the freedom and equality in the new nation, and a thumbing of the nose to old authority, according to W.J. Rorabaugh, author of *The Alcoholic Republic*.

This habit was epitomized by John L. Sullivan, a boxer dubbed the "Boston Strong Boy." One of the country's first celebrity athletes, he was a champion of the bare-knuckled bout who could brag he had won more than 450 fights. Born in Boston's South End in 1858, he won his nickname as a youth and went on to box around the country, although he often had to be dragged from a saloon for practice. He often insisted on buying rounds for the house and reportedly tried to slug a bartender who had the temerity to give him change back. Sullivan, however, eventually swore off drinking and became a temperance speaker. He died in 1918. He might be amused to know that today his name and likeness have been used to market "John L. Sullivan Irish Whiskey," introducing a next generation to this boy from Boston.

As Americans drank more, New England's temperance movement grew in fits and starts, always trying to find that elusive balance between public reform and personal liberty. Initially, the push was for moderation, rather than insisting upon strict abstinence for all. The first temperance groups, oddly enough, served many of the same functions as the corner tavern, that is, they were social outlets. As Rorabaugh writes, "Some men sought camaraderie at the tavern, others in their local temperance organization." The Commonwealth also continued its flirtation with control of alcohol, making various attempts to control the drinking habits of its citizens through the early nineteenth century, with a merry-go-round of banning, lifting, and banning. Liquor and/or beer sales were banned from 1852 to 1875 when prohibition laws were finally abandoned. In 1881, Massachusetts became the first state in the nation to institute the principle of local option in which communities could issue—or ban—licenses for the sale of intoxicating liquors. In 1910, Boston voted a resounding 54,094 to 26,972 to keep on issuing liquor licenses, although by this time most of the cities around Boston, such as Cambridge, Somerville, Medford, and Newton, were dry.

Officially, that is.

Yankee ingenuity always found ways around the law. In 1838, when Massachusetts was attempting to curtail liquor consumption, one man figured out a dodge. He painted a pig with red and black stripes and brought it to a military muster in Dedham. There, he applied for a license to show off his "rare" pig in a tent for an admittance price of six-and-a-quarter cents. At first, onlookers were reluctant to waste their money but soon the whispered word went out—not only could they see the freak of nature, but they could also have a glass of free grog! An observer noted: "Large numbers visited the strange animal and came out with smiling faces, smacking their lips with evident gratification."

As the nation would learn in the 1920s, banning liquor sales does not eliminate alcohol consumption. As of 1870, Boston had 2,584 places that illegally sold liquor, or one for every ninety-seven people. After legalization in 1875, the new license board approved 1,897 licenses, or a ratio of about one license to 180 citizens. But Massachusetts authorities were still on guard; in 1888 the state passed a law that limited the number of licenses that could be issued, on the assumption that fewer licenses meant fewer chances to drink and a more sober pubic. The ratio was set at one license per five hundred citizens; eleven years later, the total number of Boston liquor licenses was frozen at one thousand. Illegal grog shops continued to operate, catering to thirsty immigrants and other groups.

By 1898, no less than two hundred and fifty thousand of Boston's inhabitants—or fifty percent of the total population—visited a bar *every day*. They spent an average of ten cents a visit; that may not seem like much but consider: laborers then earned from $1.25 to $1.75 a day, while higher-wage jobs paid men $9 to $12 a week and women $3 to $5 a week.

"A Boston Bar: By Their Fruits, Ye Shall Know Them," Harper's Weekly, 1874. From the author's collection.

Yet overindulgence was a side effect—not necessarily the goal; even those who opposed drinking concluded that the popularity of taverns was based on "a deeper thirst for fellowship and recreation." Indeed, whether it was called a saloon, tavern, grog shop, taproom, barroom, kitchen barroom, blind pig, or gin mill, early nineteenth-century drinking establishments served as social clubs, political clubs, and affordable places to get a meal as well as a drink. They took on, as author Madelon Powers writes, "a pivotal role in the cooperative and self-organizing efforts of the emerging working class."

Powers, whose book *Faces Along the Bar*, published in 1998, explores her fascination with the social function of the country's working-class taverns, provides a description of what saloons looked like beginning in the 1870s. Hardwood floors, sometimes covered with sawdust, and a polished bar of oak or mahogany that ran nearly the length of the establishment were customary. Food—the proverbial free lunch—was often provided as another lure. It was usually very salty fare to increase thirst. A typical Boston menu might include crackers, bologna, wienerwurst, sliced tomatoes, pickles, onions, radishes, and a hot soup or stew, either provided gratis or at bargain prices. Rarely were stools or chairs provided; men leaned against the bar, with a foot on a brass rail. This served as an early warning system to bartenders. The minute a patron's foot began to miss the rail, he was cut off.

By the beginning of the twentieth century, Boston barrooms had evolved to be a social, political, and economic institution, according to Perry Duis, who published an exhaustive examination of the saloons of Boston and Chicago in 1983. Saloons were used for weddings and wakes, for meetings both private and public. They sheltered the homeless; regulars were allowed to sleep on benches or floors in return for cleanup duty. Saloonkeepers functioned as bankers, advancing money to poor clients, sometimes at unsavory rates, other times with low interest. Some were as unscrupulous as temperance workers would depict them; some were hardworking family men. "The saloon, being both a small business and essentially an extension of the sidewalk, reflected the diversity of Chicago and Boston, perhaps more than any other social institution," Duis writes.

Boston saloonkeepers were often shrewd political operatives. One even established a political dynasty. Patrick "P.J." Kennedy, the only son of a struggling Irish widow, worked on the East Boston dock and saved enough to buy a small tavern near Boston's Haymarket Square. He later bought the Maverick House hotel in East Boston and established a liquor-importing business. A Democratic ward boss the likes of James Michael Curley and Martin Lomansey, Kennedy also served in the Massachusetts House of Representatives. Reportedly, he seldom drank but he used his position as a saloonkeep to great political advantage, becoming the boss of Ward 2. Like other bar owners, he loaned money, put up bail, and provided spirits for weddings and other events. His son, Joseph Kennedy, would marry Rose Fitzgerald, the daughter of Boston mayor John "Honey Fitz" Fitzgerald and father a large family of politicians and activists, including a future president and two future senators. Thus, the Kennedy saga, it could be argued, was born in a bar.

Popular writer and humorist George Ade lauded the saloon as an American institution in his book, *The Old-Time Saloon, Not Wet, Not Dry, Just History*, much as Samuel Adams Drake revered the tavern as a birthplace for revolution decades earlier. "The saloon was the rooster crow of the spirit of democracy," Ade declares. "It may have been the home of sodden indulgence and a training school for criminality, but it had a lot of enthusiastic comrades."

Not the least of the comforts the nineteenth-century saloon afforded its patrons was a wide array of liquid options, far more sophisticated and potent than their forefathers' flips and bounces. A good bartender could put together any one of fifty cocktails "without making a false move," although most requests were for beer and whiskey. "Beer [was] for the thirsty and red liquor for those who wished to induce, for at least a brief period, the sense of well being," according to Ade. A welcome holiday concoction was the Tom and Jerry, made with brandy, eggs, nutmeg, and rum—preferably a local rum distilled just a few miles away, in Medford. From 1830 to 1905, Old Medford Rum made by Daniel Lawrence & Sons on Ship Street was considered among the nation's finest. "Apple-jack could perfume the breath, but it was mild and innocuous compared with Medford Rum," Ade observes. "Anyone who drank eight mugs of Tom and Jerry could arise the next morning and see his breath."

Americans also favored absinthe, whiskey, and gin. Sherry and Madeira were the most popular of wines, but Drake's Plantation Bitters, Boker's Stomach Bitters, Paine's Celery Compound, Ayer's Sarsaparilla (concoctions with high alcohol content), and Sweet Catawba (a wine) were popular as mixers or by themselves. Beer making, which had always been done on a small scale since Colonial Days, was also increasing as a profitable, larger-scale business. Beginning in the 1820s, breweries were built in Charlestown, South Boston, and the Jamaica Plain/Mission Hill sections of the city. These breweries supplied beer to saloons and taverns dotting the city; additionally, major American brewing companies—Pabst, Schlitz, Anheuser, and Busch—sought partnership with saloons through distribution contracts and helped to promote the opening of new bars. In return, bars agreed to serve only one brand of beer, a lucrative arrangement for both parties.

Saloons weren't the only institutions catering to the drinking class. Hotels and restaurants satisfied the thirst for wines and fancier drinks. Institutions like the Parker House (built on School Street in downtown Boston in 1854 by Harvey D. Parker of the aforementioned Parker's), the Hotel Vendome, Touraine, and Marliave mixed fine dining with even finer drinking. From 1896 to 1911, about eighty percent of all liquor dealers in Boston were hotels or restaurants.

Waves of Irish immigration that would eventually move the city's power structure away from the English Brahmin class were followed by Italians, Germans, Jews from Russia and Poland, and Portuguese. These immigrants soon created their versions of the neighborhood bar, which fast became an important source of recreation and amusement for new Americans. Here men could read an Old World newspaper, hear live entertainment, or get the latest sporting news by ticker tape. Boston's inner city dwellers often had few other options for recreation; parks were often located far from working-class neighborhoods and the system of public swimming pools drew fewer people than taverns, even in the sweltering heat. Saloons and other neighborhood bars incubated both politicians and political movements. Meanwhile, voters were treated to rounds of drinks provided by candidates or were influenced by the saloon owners as to who would make the best candidate. "The saloon is...the place where political opinion is formed very quickly," says Robert A. Woods, the editor of two studies of immigrant populations in Boston. "Other things being equal, the man who has the greater number of saloonkeepers on his side will surely be elected." Lest this seem quaint, think of today's political discourse when pundits ask voters penetrating questions such as, "Which candidate would you prefer to have a drink with?"

Taverns introduced immigrants to American life while allowing them to celebrate their heritage from the old country. Irish bars celebrated St. Patrick's Day, elevating the holiday far greater than ever celebrated on the Emerald Isle. In the North End, the Italian community drank beer as well as traditional wine and, because playing cards was outlawed, played games with their fingers. Woods observes: "The Italians, though they are beginning to drift into the American saloons, patronize chiefly the saloons of their own people. These are situated on North Street and one or two adjoining streets, and are resorted to for social as well as drinking purposes. Indeed, gaming rather than drinking seems to be their chief attraction. A man buys a glass of light wine or beer, and sitting down at one of the little tables, with which these saloons are well supplied, passes two or three hours in some game of chance with his companions, or in watching the play that may be going on." Continuing, Woods reveals the era's prejudice: "There are a few Jewish and Italian liquor sellers, but the Irish still hold their regrettable monopoly of that noxious trade. The saloons are the last commercial relic of Irish occupation." He describes one particular saloon above a North End "rat pit" where "drinks were served by girls with painted cheeks and in low-necked dresses." Ah, the horror.

WORKING A SUCKER IN A CONCERT-SALOON

Courtesy of the Trustees of the Boston Public Library.

Despite Woods's shocking descriptions, Boston's bars were by all accounts more controlled and reserved places compared to those in Chicago and New York. Pool tables were allowed in pool halls, only rarely in taverns. Prostitution and gambling were nearly entirely divorced from saloons. Boston barrooms were not, Duis also argues, necessarily all-male places, even if legally women were forbidden to drink there. Often the proprietor's wife helped out behind the bar, and German saloons were family-oriented institutions. Women were arrested for public drunkenness at a far lower rate than men, but they were arrested, implying that they were tippling like their male counterparts and sometimes suffering the consequences as well. But in the 1890s women were forbidden by police regulation to patronize barrooms and often were turned away by the sign "No drinks sold to ladies."

And yet some Boston women did frequent saloons, and not a few were from the upper classes. In February 1894, an intrepid female reporter from the *Boston Globe* spent two evenings in the saloons of Boston from the North End to downtown to explore the phenomenon, publishing her observations in a lengthy article. "Women drink," she concludes. "At least some women drink. It is an unpleasant subject to think about or see in black and white or meet practically illustrated, but any observer of the passing show has to admit it is terribly true."

This unnamed scribe claims to have discretely poured the contents of her beverages into cuspidors and out open windows when no one was looking, presumably to keep her edge. While in the North End, she observed a young girl filling a pail of booze—a growler—to bring home to the family, a common custom at the time. At a Fleet Street establishment, she was astonished to see that the head bartender was a woman "and such a clever one, I could hardly keep my eyes from her to look at anything else." At this saloon, she also found a "gay party of young girls" with escorts hovering nearby, as well as two toothless "old crones" drinking hot whiskey and touching everyone who came near them for a drink. A rosy-cheeked German barmaid, the wife of the owner, worked so quickly "her fingers seemed to have wings."

Later that evening, she visited an "Italian hotel" with a café and bar, filled with an equal number of men and women. She ate a delicious bowl of soup, choked on the cigar smoke, and watched as women young and old drank, laughed, gossiped, swore a few times, and even stood a round to the waiter. She saw what she would call respectable women and women who "might be classed in another category."

On she ventured, to a "swell" bar on Washington Street, known for catering to women. It took her a while to find her way down a narrow, dark alley to the rear of the building where there was an entrance reserved for females, but once inside she found a waiter who brought her into a large hall reserved for women and their escorts. She ordered a Manhattan and a glass of ale ("as I saw there would be plenty of chance to dispose of them") and proceeded to chat up women sitting near her. There were husbands and wives, but also women with each other, including one with her ten- or twelve-year-old daughter. To the reporter's eye, all these women appeared dignified and independent; "Their gowns were well made, their bonnets were tasteful, and expensive fur-trimmed wraps were flung over the backs of their chairs." One of them even sent her daughter to the bar to ask the man to send over a couple of beers and rewarded the girl with a taste when they came. The scribe also recognized the wife of a shoe merchant, who downed a brandy with one gulp; at that moment she understood why the tip of her nose was always blushed.

Her evening ended at midnight in the West End at an unlicensed bar. Now at ease, she asked the bartender to join her. The well-dressed, clean-shaven gentleman brought over two whiskeys. His family lived on the first floor, and he admitted women every night but Saturday, when there were too many sailors. He said he would like to be licensed, but he was not making enough to afford the legal fees. "No my dear lady, I can afford the risks better than a license."

This female reporter—as well as her friends—would have been welcome at one of Boston's most venerable drinking establishments, founded by a German immigrant. Jacob Wirth was born in Kreuznach, Prussia, into a family of winegrowers. In 1868, after moving to the United States, he opened a restaurant called Jacob Wirth's at 60 Eliot Street, later renamed Stuart Street, and in 1878 he moved it across the street to where it stands today at 31-37 Stuart Street. From a long mahogany bar, Wirth and his waiters served up drinks and special dishes including sausages, pig's knuckles, boiled bacon, hams, cheeses, and herrings. A Latin motto graced the wall: *Suum Cuique*. To Each His Own. In addition to selling imported Rhine wine, Wirth was the Boston agent for Anheuser-Busch Brewing Company and George Ehret's New York Hell Gate Lager. The *Boston Globe* described him as "the first man to engage extensively in bottling beer for family use." Reportedly, when barrels of beer were unloaded from a ramp, Wirth would catch the edge of the barrel with his foot, causing it to stop and spin. Boston Strong Boy John L. Sullivan—a regular—was fascinated by this trick, but when he tried it, he was knocked flat on his back, which was a bit of an embarrassment for the boxer.

Wirth died in 1892, and his son, also named Jacob Wirth, took over the business after dropping out from Harvard. The younger Jake was a beloved figure in Boston, eulogized as "the artisan who blended hearty German food, dark beer worthy of a man's time, and flowing sawdust underneath unpretentious mahogany tables into a human

*Beer haulers outside Jacob Wirth Co. Restaurant,
from the booklet* A Seidel for Jake Wirth.

experience." A tall, impeccably dressed man with steel gray hair and clipped mustache, he maintained the bar the way Bostonians liked it—mostly unchanged—for sixty years. His restaurant was considered an eminently respectable establishment of high moral tone. For years it was well known for its sign "Ladies are requested not to smoke," which was not removed until the 1970s. The request was strictly enforced—even a Radcliffe student who declined to put out her cigarette in 1923 was politely asked to leave. The waiter patiently explained to her and her male companion that this was an effort to keep out loose women, who would kill time between pick-ups by smoking.

While many bars and saloons were divided by ethnic identity and class, Jacob Wirth's had a more universal appeal. "Young veterans gathered to chew over Gettysburg and Chancellorsville and wash down their rugged memories with foaming freshets of dark brew... Here you will find a burly truck driver in shirt sleeves dissecting a pig's knuckle alongside two young members of the Massachusetts Institute of Technology faculty sticking the conversational knife and fork into a problem of outer space." This colorful description comes from a 1989 booklet about the bar called *A Seidel for Jake Wirth*; "seidel" is a German word for beer mug.

Jacob Wirth's restaurant survived Prohibition, but only by serving "near beer" that had an alcohol content under the legal limit of one-half of one percent. Wirth died in 1965 at age eighty-five, still active in the restaurant business. Services were held in the First Church of Boston. As the *Boston Globe* noted, "If the First Church had never heard the word 'beer' inside its great sophistication, it heard it well during the eulogy. The word carried a rich and delicate meaning all its own." His restaurant, now under different management, continues to serve drinks and food to this day.

Another "respectable" bar was the Bell in Hand Tavern, which operated for as many as seventy years on Williams Court—also called Pi (or Pie) Alley—in downtown Boston. Tales about its conception have taken the form of legend, and the facts are murky. According to The Bostonian Society, the wooden Bell in Hand sign, etched with the date 1795, was used to mark a business on Eliot Street run by the town crier. The business was later taken over by a succeeding town crier, James Wilson. A dewy-eyed account of Wilson written by the Reverend Edward Griffin Porter in *Rambles in Old Boston, New England* published in 1886, reports that "Jimmy" Wilson, a brush maker by trade, was once the best-known person in Old Boston. He was a short, thickset, red-faced man with keen eyes and a powerful voice (although how Porter knew this is baffling). According to Porter and other sources, Wilson sold ale along with brushes, possibly in the basement of the City Exchange on Congress and Devonshire streets, once the site of the Exchange Coffee Shop, which was an eating and drinking establishment. Outside he hung the bell in hand sign, as a symbol of his position as town crier. Wilson also used the steps of the Exchange Coffee Shop to announce auctions. By various accounts, Wilson was a humorous, jovial man, with a quick wit and a handy comeback to those who gathered to hear him. His custom was to appear on the street, ring a bell three times, and then announce the news of the day, ranging from a missing cow to a lost boy. "His account of the agony of bereaved parents would be heart-rending, when he would suddenly explode a joke which would start the crowd off, roaring," writes Porter. Wilson died in 1841, and his bell in hand sign was moved to Williams Court to be used for a tavern of the same name, which opened, as much as can be determined, in the 1850s. By 1886, the Bell in Hand, or "Bell" as it was affectionately known, was a Boston landmark.

Illustration of the Bell in Hand Tavern, from the author's collection.

The Bell in Hand in the 1880s was a chummy, English-style pub with sawdust on the floor and tobacco smoke so thick it was hard to see a vacant chair, according to Robert Earle May, writing in the 1911 edition of the magazine *Caledonian* (devoted to all things Scottish.) No ardent spirits were served, some even called it a "temperance bar," but hearty ale was provided in pewter mugs along with mutton pie and other delights of English cuisine. The walls were covered with engravings, oil paintings, lithographs, and woodcut etchings. Here, May overheard a prominent Boston politician thump the table and exclaim, "I don't give a *blank* how much a man steals from the city, if he is personally *honest*." (A slogan that could have been applied to any number of politicians at the time.) "There is a spirit of camaraderie here," May continues, "no drunken loafer will touch you for a drink, but you will likely be offered one for the sake of companionship or good cheer and you must be gentle in your refusal." A photo, circa 1890, of the Bell in Hand Tavern shows waiters in starched white coats and ties, standing stiff but proud beside and behind a polished wooden bar. Pewter cups hang neatly behind them, and demure portraits gaze out from the walls.

The Bell was popular among the city's literary set and likely among reporters from the *Boston Herald* and *Boston Globe*, which had offices nearby. Ralph Adams Cram, who would win fame as an architect, was a frequent visitor, writing in his memoirs that "one whiff of its unique atmosphere transported one back into the eighteenth century." It was here at a "serious but not altogether sober party," that Cram and others came up with an idea for the literary journal *The Mahogany Tree*, the magazine that first published Willa Cather.

The Bell in Hand Tavern, 1883. Courtesy of the Bostonian Society.

Although the Bell in Hand didn't serve hard spirits, it was but an island in a sea of watering holes. By any standard, Boston was choc-a-block with bars. An 1884 temperance map found eighty-one bars in the areas bounded by Albany Street, Kneeland Street, Federal Street, and East Street, in what is now in the Leather District, near South Station. An 1886 map produced by another temperance group identified ninety-five saloons ranging "from the gilded gin mill to the dive" in the blocks around Boston City Hall, then located between School and Court streets.

The Bell in Hand Tavern, 1891. Courtesy of Historic New England.

The two South End Settlement House studies, published in 1898 and 1903, reported about one hundred barrooms in the South End, about eighty-eight in the West End, and ninety-seven in the North End, most of which were patronized by non-residents from dry communities.

Boston was an eager participant in what modern drink mavens consider the golden age of cocktails. A bartender for the Adams House hotel on Washington Street rhapsodically listed the most popular libations for a *Boston Globe* reporter in November 1927: the House's famous (and potent) punch, mixed daily; Ward Eights; a variety of highballs, various fizzes, and Tom Collinses; brandy egg nogs; Mamie Taylors; Tom and Jerrys; spiced rums, toddies, sours, and cobblers. Bartender Walter Sutton also described serving juleps, smashes, and rickeys, as well as champagne, burgundies, and sherries.

It was a time of ingenuity with spirits. An 1862 drinking manual written by famed bartender Jerry Thomas, the first of its kind in the United States, features an astounding amount of recipes for various punches, slings, crustas, flips, and other libations.

This was the era that produced the now-popular Aviation, Between the Sheets, and the Sidecar. "Bartenders were very much involved in popular culture and wanted to stay in conversation with their regulars," says Boston bartender John Gertsen. "If there was this new thing cropping up like flying, they would want to stay on top of it. It was actually very popular in that period, the early twentieth century, to have cocktails named after famous plays, works of art, actors." Hence the Maiden's Blush, the Mary Pickford, and the Rob Roy.

But the era was not golden for all. Saloons were feared—and not without cause—as places where men drank up their paychecks and where they became violent with inebriation, often taking it out on their families at home. The temperance movement, looming on the horizon, turned that unease into political action.

Moreover, in the nineteenth and early twentieth century, Boston's drinking was increasingly segmented by social class and ethnic background. Whereas Judge Sewall could hold court in a tavern and later sit down for a drink with owner George Monk, Boston's upper classes associated public drinking with the perceived vices of the immigrant poor.

As late as 1895, the Back Bay—one of Boston's poshest neighborhoods— lacked a public saloon. The wealthy didn't need these public watering holes for socializing as did their Colonial-era forbearers. If immigrants had their saloons, Boston's elite drank in elegant hotels or at their clubs— exclusive organizations like the Algonquin, Union, St. Botolph, Somerset, and Tavern clubs—many of which survive to this day. The Tavern Club, established in 1884, was considered one of the more "artsy" of these male bastions (today women can join), and members included eminent Bostonians who, if they were not temperance supporters, certainly mingled with those who were among the leaders of the movement. Meetings were, however, anything but dry; take the ditty composed by Winthrop Ames, for the club's "Lawyer's Night" on February 3, 1902:

Every worthy club in Boston
Has its proper point of pride:
At the Botolph Sunday Concerts,
At the Somerset 't is "side."
And the graveyard gives the Union
Its distinctive clammy calm,
But the Dry Martini Cocktail
Is the Tavern's special charm!
OH!
Take a pinch of pepper,
Add a gill of ink,
Half a rubber overshoe:
Mix 'em in the sink.
Stew 'em in a saucepan
Top 'em off with ale. ...
That's the Tavern mixture
For a Dry Cocktail.

The sons of the wealthy also drank with gusto. The Bostonian Society has in its collection the Minutes of The Outcast Club, an arch recounting of meetings from 1886 to 1887 of four or five Harvard students who spent an inordinate amount of time calculating the price of beer. On September 20, 1887, these high-spirited gents got a comedown; Cambridge exercised its local option to go dry. The minutes record that "On the first day of May, a terrible curse fell upon the fair city of Cambridge and fell most heavily of all upon this club. The common herd of the city voted in town election that for one year from May 1, 1887 to May 1, 1888, there should be no liquor stronger than three percent belly wash sold in town. This necessitated a change of policy in the method of procuring our beer. It was deemed most expedient and best by our agents Johnson and Doane that we should procure our malt extract from Boston by express. The expressage was fifteen cents per case and this unlooked for drain upon the club treasury soon swallowed up the Sinking Fund."

As went Cambridge, so would go the nation. But like so much about alcohol, Boston continued to operate with a dual standard, distinguishing between the gin mills where "they" drink and the fine establishment where "we" drink. A cartoon highlighting this duality was published in a liquor industry publication, *Mida's Criterion*, on March 1, 1909. The cartoon shows a foppish man in an elite club raising his glass to declare: "The Saloon with the free lunch for the unemployed should be driven out and communities made dry. But CLUBS of our standing with private lockers should be privileged to remain."

From the vantage point of a century, however, it's clear that entrenched prejudices muddied the waters of rational debate about alcoholism in Boston. Certainly, as Powers writes, the saloon's role "in aggravating alcoholism, disease, violent crime, family hardship, job absenteeism, political corruption, and other social problems has been well documented. (But) despite the saloon's faults and excesses, however, it earned considerable customer loyalty by serving as both shelter and staging ground for its vast working-class clientele."

As immigration continued, Boston's old Yankee upper class reacted with attitudes ranging from mild concern to systematized opposition, such as the organization of the Immigration Restriction League of 1894. Drinking was associated with the bad habits of "invading hordes" of Irish, Germans, and Italians, seen as a threat to the dignified tone of New England life. This is not to suggest there was no heartfelt concern on the part of reformers for the poor who were increasingly packing inner cities and who suffered from a host of social ills. There were many who saw alcohol as the cause of poverty, not a symptom of it. However, it is striking that, when reading the reams of books, pamphlets, and articles decrying the saloon in Boston, there is no naming of names, per se. Alcohol is singled out, but not the establishment where it was served nor those who sold it. Rather, New Englanders took a typically New England approach: Form a committee. The Committee of Fifty was a prestigious group of university administrators, scholars, and tradesmen—members included Harvard President Charles W. Eliot and Harvard professor and physician Francis G. Peabody—which was convened from 1893 to 1903 to "study the Liquor Problem in the hope of securing a body of facts which may serve as a basis for intelligent and private action." The committee made an exhaustive study of liquor use in the United States and ultimately concluded that while drinking in general was bad for the populace, the saloon was not necessarily a den of unmitigated evil: "The fact that the saloon is more than a mere drinking place and that it supplies many legitimate wants besides the craving for intoxication, should be frankly recognized and ought to be of help to those who are engaged in practical efforts to counteract the evils of

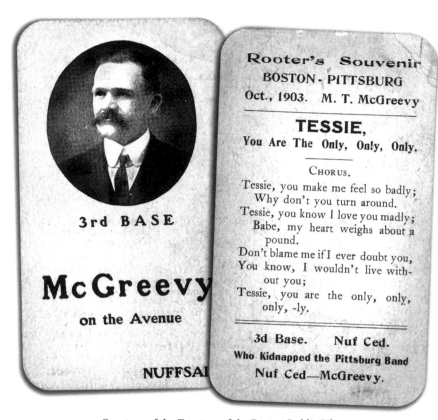

intemperance." The committee attempted to come up with alternatives to the saloon but had to acknowledge that none emerged to match the allure of this home away from home. What could, for example, compete with Michael "Nuf Ced" McGreevy's saloon?

For thirty years, McGreevy ran a sports bar business to which all other sports bars owe homage. Born on June 16, 1865 in Roxbury to an Irish immigrant day laborer and Roxbury native, McGreevy established a bar in 1894 at 940 Columbus Avenue. An athletic man, McGreevy was a decent amateur ball player, a regular handball player, and coach for the "Nuf Ced" Roxbury team. Newspapers of the day often published photos of him jumping into Boston Harbor in the winter for a regular swim, doing handstands, or ice-skating bare-chested for crowds. Ironically, McGreevy himself may have been either a teetotaler or a light drinker. His liquor business and bar seemed to only serve his real passion in life.

McGreevy led a group called the Roxbury Rooters, which evolved into the Royal Rooters, and who eventually swore allegiance verging on obsession to the Boston Red Sox. McGreevy, and often Mayor John "Honey Fitz" Fitzgerald, led the Rooters to the Huntington Avenue Grounds ballpark and later to Fenway Park to cheer lustily and sing their anthem, "Tessie." McGreevy was so devoted, he often traveled to out-of-town games. In 1908, McGreevy promised a diamond ring to the best base runner, and the next spring he handed one to player Amby McConnell.

In October 1915, McGreevy moved his bar to property on Tremont Street at the corner of Ruggles Street, essentially recreating the tavern from Columbus Avenue. A life-size statue known as "Baseball Man," with a regulation baseball uniform and Boston written across his chest, was installed over the doorway. Baseball Man was a welcoming sight whether the hometown team won or lost.

Baseball was—and remains—a great leveler in Boston society. If McGreevy's raucous hordes cheered for the Red Sox, well, so did Mrs. Isabella Stewart Gardner, a prominent member of Boston society, whose home and art collection would become the famed Gardner Museum. In 1912, Mrs. Jack scandalized her peers by wearing a headband emblazoned with "Oh You Red Sox"—the title of a popular song—at a proper Boston Symphony Orchestra performance. At least that's the legend; but Mrs. Jack was a known fan who bought season tickets at Fenway and kept news items and photos of the team in her scrapbooks. It's likely she never made an appearance at McGreevy's Third Base, but she shared the passion of the patrons.

But a great dry wave was coming that would halt the era of the Boston saloon. The Red Sox would win the World Series in 1918, but McGreevy was canny enough to realize that baseball enthusiasm alone would not run a tavern if Prohibition was passed. As a man of moderation, he argued that the soft liquors—beer and wine—should be allowed and that this would resolve issues better than a complete ban. To no avail. Believing that Prohibition would be long-lived, he closed his Third Base saloon in 1920. Still generous in spirit, he donated his baseball photographs to the Boston Public Library, and the collection remains a crown jewel in the library's holdings. By 1923, the Tremont Street location had been leased and turned into a branch of the Boston Public Library. Now, as a library newsletter put it, "books will be dispensed instead of beer, the morning paper instead of a pick-me-up."

McGreevy retired from the bar business and remained a baseball fan, if a less prominent one, as the Royal Rooters disbanded. He lived to see Prohibition repealed, but he died in February 1943 without seeing another World Series victory by the Red Sox. In 2004, the Irish punk rock band Dropkick Murphys released a new version of "Tessie," working in McGreevy's name. After eighty-six dry years, the Sox won the series. Then, in 2008, after yet another World Series win, Dropkick Murphys leader Ken Casey joined forces with producer and baseball historian Peter Nash to launch a new McGreevy's sports bar at 911 Boylston Street, using a replica of the original Third Base that was used as a movie set.

'Nuff said.

BRONX COCKTAIL

1 ½ ounces dry gin
¾ ounce dry vermouth
¾ ounce sweet vermouth
Fresh juice of ¼ orange

Shake well with cracked ice and strain
into a cocktail glass.

Serve with slice of orange.

Woman's Holy War, Currier & Ives lithograph, courtesy of the Library of Congress, Prints & Photographs Division.

PROHIBITION, PART I: SO LONG, JOHN BARLEYCORN

There was three men come out o' the west their fortunes for to try,
And these three men made a solemn vow, John Barleycorn must die,
They ploughed, they sowed, they harrowed him in, throwed clods upon his head,
And these three men made a solemn vow, John Barleycorn was dead.

—English folk song

Poor old John Barleycorn. The English folk character who represented distilled spirits and had come to stand for drinking in America was doomed to die at midnight of January 16, 1920. Boston made sure he had a proper send off. Hundreds of people thronged bars, hotels, and restaurants to drink a final toast to J.B. and to the act of toasting itself. Wakes were held in hotels. Mock coffins were filled with empties as men mourned and women wailed. Waiters wore black caps and crepe. "To the clink of flasks, the popping of champagne corks, and voices raised in song, John Barleycorn was given a long-to-be remembered farewell by his devotees," said the *Boston Post*. Not to be outdone, the *Boston Herald* reported, "With weird ceremonies, and amid bacchanalian revels, laughter, song, and dance, the last hours of J. Barleycorn were celebrated last night and early this morning by thousands of people in the hotels and restaurants of the city, and a bigger business was reported in some than even at New Year's."

While the advocates of the Eighteenth Amendment heartily—and soberly—celebrated, Boston's newspapers treated the advent of Prohibition with a wink, as if this were all a good joke: Prohibition would surely become one of those odd Puritan laws that remained on the books but was not actually enforced. Seeking a sensational quote, the wags of the *Boston Evening Record* contacted Billy Sunday, the fiery evangelist and prominent dry preacher of Norfolk, Virginia, to get his reaction to what they called "John Barleycorn's Black Friday, the Sober Sixteenth of January." Sunday did not disappoint: "The Prohibition amendment will hold down the population of hell. The devil is preparing to bank his fires, put crepe on the door, and hand out the 'For Rent' sign."

The jocular tone of the Boston coverage, demonstrated in editorials and cartoons, was tempered only by a sense of resignation. Revelers were festive but orderly; there were only about twenty arrests on January 16, 1920, as Bostonians seemed to accept the inevitable. But, Prohibition, let's recall, did not actually ban the private use of alcohol. The rich could keep their cellars of aging wine or bottles of port, which could be served to guests without fear of a knock at the door. Spirits for medicinal purposes—there still being a perception that alcohol was good for a body on some occasions—could still be sold. Only the poor and the unconnected were truly affected, as they could no longer (legally) belly up to the bar or stop in at the local saloon for a quick one.

The *Boston Post* spelled out the complicated rules: You couldn't drink except in a private residence; you couldn't have liquor in your club or hotel unless you lived there and kept it locked up; you couldn't carry a hip flask; and you couldn't buy fruit juice after it started to ferment. If you were ill, you could get a doctor's prescription for alcohol filled at the drug store, provided that the prescription was for no more than one pint every ten days. However, you could keep liquor in your home and serve it as freely as you liked to your family and guests. And, the male writer for the *Post* added, your wife could cook with it freely—should "you want to waste it that way."

But the jokes quickly grew stale, and some Bostonians saw trouble on the horizon about this new law. "Who's going to do the arresting?" they asked reporters.

The reporters shrugged. Who indeed?

Illegal booze seized in a raid.
Courtesy of the Trustees of the Boston Public Library.

The political path that led to the wake of John Barleycorn was a long one and cut a broad swath through New England. In fact, temperance activity in the United States was primarily concentrated in the Northeast until 1830, with New England accounting for a third of all affiliated groups. For many, the push against spirits began as an argument of rationality, not morality. While the Puritans and early American leaders frowned on drunkenness, moderate use of spirits was considered not only proper but beneficial. Drink was a gift from God, to be used moderately. Yet there was some inkling that starting the morning with a tankard of ale, in the habit of John Adams, might not be a healthy breakfast of champions. Founding Father and physician Benjamin Rush began to suspect that spirits were harmful to health, far more harmful than wine or beer. In 1784, he penned an influential pamphlet entitled "An Inquiry into the Effects of Ardent Spirits on the Human Mind and Body" that would shape temperance thought for decades. While Rush did not advocate abstinence, he argued that weaker liquor such as beer was healthier than distilled liquor. Historian W. J. Rorabaugh called Rush's work a "masterpiece" in its measured use of scientific ideals, logic, and specific examples, saying it reflected Enlightenment views that rational, reasoned arguments, soberly presented, could change minds and improve behavior. By 1850, more than 170,000 copies had been circulated.

Rush's arguments profoundly impacted Jeremy Belknap, a prominent Boston minister and historian who later founded the Massachusetts Historical Society. Both Belknap and Rush attempted to strip away the old Puritan arguments about the immorality of inebriation and replace them with a reasoned appeal that no matter how good grog made you feel, it was bad for your physical well-being. Their approach was radical; in the early- to mid-1700s, many elites believed that working-class men simply would not perform their jobs without alcohol, either as a kind of quasi-payment (as seen in the allotment of rum and spirits given to sailors) or to ease the strain of back-breaking labor.

Nonetheless, the sentiment that alcohol should be controlled by civic authorities in some fashion was soon part of the mindset of the Commonwealth's lawmakers. Massachusetts tried various approaches, both carrot and stick. In the 1780s, the Massachusetts legislature exempted brewery equipment from property taxes to encourage less potent beer making instead of distilled spirits. In 1838, the legislature adopted the "fifteen-gallon law," which mandated that a person could buy no less than fifteen gallons of spirits at one time—the belief being that citizens would neither have the money to buy such an amount of alcohol, nor the means to transport it. This ill-conceived law, which in effect only penalized the poor, was repealed in 1840 and was ridiculed for decades as one of the state's do-gooder laws run amok.

Raid on a still in South Boston.
Courtesy of the Trustees of the Boston Public Library.

In 1813, the Massachusetts Society for the Suppression of Intemperance was formed with the idea of encouraging citizens to strengthen their will to resist temptation for strong drink. About fourteen years later, sixteen temperance leaders met in Boston to form the American Society for the Promotion of Temperance, later known as the American Temperance Society. In 1838, delegations from various societies met in Boston and formed the Massachusetts Temperance Union, whose members pledged to abstain entirely from the use of all intoxicating liquors. The area was soon awash with all kinds of temperance organizations, many serving as social clubs.

"Secret" teetotaler societies similar to Masons were formed; the Temperance Watchmen had two clubs in Boston in the 1850s. Members of these clubs not only pledged to keep liquor from their lips but to actively discourage the manufacture, sale, and use of alcoholic beverages. Befitting its position as the nation's literary soul, dozens of temperance newspapers and journals appeared in Boston. *The Boston Spy*, which claimed to be the only weekly newspaper in the state devoted to temperance, launched in 1840 with the motto, "Without Fear, Without Favor."

It's vital to clear up a popular misconception: The temperance movement in New England did not start as a push to ban alcohol in its entirety. Rather, the movement evolved, as advocates moved from promoting moderation to total abstinence to stringent controls of liquor sales and manufacturing. The Reverend William Ellery Channing, considered the father of Unitarianism and celebrated for his anti-slavery and liberal religious views—and whose statue stands in a corner of the Public Garden—in 1837 nonetheless admonished the Massachusetts Temperance Society: "What ought not to be used as a beverage, ought not to be sold as such. What the good of the community requires us to expel, no man has a moral right to sell." Upping the ante, the Total Abstinence Party was formed in 1841, although one of their meetings in Faneuil Hall in 1847 was broken up by "rum rowdies" who rushed the stage and struck organizer John B. Gould in the head with a chair. "This is in Boston! This is in Faneuil Hall!" he tried to shout over the din. When order was finally restored, Gould apparently made an eloquent speech.

Boston banned the sale of liquor in 1847 when Mayor Josiah Quincy, Jr., broke a tie among the Boston Board of Aldermen on the issue of licensing retail liquor sellers. To the north, Maine passed a notorious law in 1851 that prohibited the sale of all alcohol except for "medicinal, mechanical, or manufacturing purposes." The act gave rise to the term "bootlegger," which referred to the smuggling of liquor to thirsty woodsmen in boots hidden by pants legs. In 1852, Massachusetts attempted to curtail alcohol sales along with other states; the Supreme Judicial Court threw out the Massachusetts law in 1854, citing constitutional concerns about search and seizures. Eventually in 1875, local communities were given the power to regulate alcohol.

The political divisions of nineteenth-century Boston should not be viewed through the prism of today's left-right, conservative-progressive divide. Opposition to alcohol consumption reflected the growing Yankee distrust of the new waves of immigrants—Irish, Italian, and Eastern European—that were transforming the city. Even leaders of the abolition movement were virulently against "foreign" newcomers, and they often singled out the Irish for their "lazy, drinking" ways. The emergence of the workingman's saloon underscores this concern. Prominent progressive thinkers agitated against alcohol, including writer Louisa May Alcott, abolitionist firebrand William Lloyd Garrison, and the Reverend Edward Everett Hale, the author of the famed short story "The Man Without A Country."

Officers smashing seized casks of illegal alcohol.
Courtesy of the Trustees of the Boston Public Library.

Temperance issues were mostly pushed aside during the 1850s as the nation was convulsed with the moral issue of slavery, culminating in the Civil War. But by the 1870s, the tone and thrust of temperance had moved from the rationality of persuasion to the outright insistence that a dry country was a better country. Prominent Bostonians like Henry Cushing argued that "the public good is the supreme law." Liberty should be granted to unpopular religious sects and newspapers, he conceded, but if, for example, a sect "lessened production, increased taxation, corrupted the ballot, deprived one tenth of the people of proper food, fuel, shelter, and clothing...the public good would justify," and "make it the duty of the law-making power to snuff out the sect or party if it could." Thus, alcohol should be curtailed for the good of all.

Not every temperance advocate took this position. Dr. Dioclesian Lewis, a prominent temperance leader, homeopath, physician, and exercise champion who had settled in Boston, declared himself personally opposed to drinking and condemned it as a poison "that should not be taken into the stomach in any form." Yet he published a massive entreaty in 1875 aimed at fellow temperance advocates that called on them to eschew legislative solutions, insisting that consumption of alcohol had plummeted in Boston and that "dependence on law was an incubus that must be shaken off." His book contained a spirited, but respectful exchange of letters with Cushing, in which Lewis argues that "nothing invades individual rights except in cases of great necessity" and drinking does not rise to the level of public danger as would a conflagration.

Francis Parkman, a historian and a member of a prominent Boston Brahmin clan, also made a far-sighted prediction. In "An Open Letter to a Temperance Friend," published posthumously in 1895 by the Massachusetts Association Opposed to the Further Extension of Suffrage to Women (Parkman opposed universal suffrage while favoring temperance), he insisted that reformers who brought about a ban on alcohol were not only doomed to fail but would also subject cities "to the corrupting face of a prohibition, which does not prohibit...prevent or even diminish drunkenness, but which is the fruitful parent of meanness, fraud, lying, and contempt of law."

But rational arguments against Prohibition were being brushed aside in a growing political movement that sought to demonize liquor manufacturers, breweries, and saloonkeepers as preying on the weak-willed and groups of immigrants. In 1870, the stakes grew higher again, with the launch of the Massachusetts Prohibition Party. Former abolitionist Wendell Phillips, an advocate of rights for women and Native Americans and whose statue is also in Boston's Public Garden, was its candidate for governor. By 1884, the Massachusetts Chapter of the Prohibition Party could support a full slate of candidates for Congress, governor, and attorney general. Temperance also began to attract women in greater numbers. While women's rights and temperance are often inextricably linked in the public mind, forward-thinking Boston women only began to participate in the temperance movement as late as the 1870s, with the organization of a chapter of the Women's Christian Temperance Union. When the Women's Christian Temperance Union partnered with the Massachusetts Prohibitory and Equal Suffrage League, membership spiked.

Indeed, the anti-alcohol battle would continue its march to both the ballot box and schoolyard. Boston women were at the forefront.

Mary Hanchett Hunt, born on the Fourth of July in 1830 in Salisbury, Connecticut, married, taught school, and later moved to the Boston area. At age forty-eight, she was asked by Frances Willard of the influential Women's Christian Temperance Union to head up the WCTU's

"Department of Scientific Temperance Instruction." Hunt would visit school boards to ask that temperance issues be incorporated in regular school courses. Dissatisfied with slow results, Hunt pushed for the election of temperance candidates who would in turn require schools to teach temperance; the WCTU would monitor compliance.

There was something about this Mary. Despite her age and modest background, she proved to be a brilliant lobbyist and by 1900, every state had passed laws mandating teaching about the evils of alcohol in public schools. Moreover, Hunt and members of the WCTU dictated the content of the instruction.

Hunt's political acumen was, however, matched by her willingness to attribute to alcohol every possible health hazard, very often to the point of utter absurdity. She promoted "facts" such as: alcohol, when it passes down the throat, burns off skin. The majority of beer drinkers die of dropsy. Many men and women are insane due to drinking problems of their parents, which they inherited. She even told the author of a children's health book to insert the claim that a single drink of liquor seriously affected one's vision. Her aim was clear: she wanted "trained haters of alcohol to pour a whole Niagara of ballots upon the saloon." Impervious to ridicule and convinced of her righteousness, Hunt attracted supporters; and by the turn of the century, Hunt had shaken up the world of public education with her insistence on temperance instruction, however dubious.

When Hunt died in Dorchester on April 24, 1906, it was discovered she had deposited royalties from her endorsements into the account of her organization, the Scientific Temperance Association. Both her heirs and the WCTU claimed the money, and the financial tangle cast a pall over her legacy. Putting things right fell to Hunt's personal secretary, Cora Frances Stoddard.

Stoddard tried to carry on Hunt's work—but in a far more meaningful way. To settle the funds issue, she helped found the Scientific Temperance Federation in Boston on December 18, 1906, and ran it for the next thirty years. The Federation's mission was to "collect and disseminate [in popular form] the result of biological, medical, social, statistical and other scientific investigations on the relations of alcoholic drink to the individual and public health." Under Stoddard's leadership, temperance advocates adopted new methods of popularizing scientific facts using charts with color diagrams, "lantern" shows (equivalent to today's PowerPoint presentations), and a traveling exhibit of models, called "Education on Wheels." Stoddard reached out to temperance movements in other counties, and in 1919, she became a member of the executive committee of the World League Against Alcoholism. Stoddard continued Hunt's work on textbooks, mended bridges with the WCTU, and very soon was engaged in the work that was nearest to her heart: actual research. Not the medical mumbo-jumbo favored by her former employer, but research harking back to the work of Benjamin Rush that would stand up against the arguments of the drippiest Wet. Moral responsibility was important, Stoddard declared, but should be "backed by more thorough understanding of what liquor and the consumption of liquor actually involved."

Stoddard was given a chance to try to test the arguments of Boston temperance advocates in the country's most celebrated "Noble Experiment." Political tides were turning against the Wets. The powerful Anti-Saloon League, with the commanding Wayne Wheeler as its voice, was organized in Ohio in 1893, and Massachusetts soon had its own chapter. In December 1913, the WCTU and the Anti-Saloon League led a march on Washington, D.C., to push for a constitutional amendment banning alcohol. By 1916, nineteen states had banned

Portrait of Cora Stoddard, from the author's collection.

the sale and manufacturing of alcohol; many speculate that children indoctrinated with temperance principles by Mary Hunt's education effort were now old enough to vote and had, indeed, turned a stream of support into that Niagara.

Yet, the Boston approach to abstinence, which favored rational argument over belligerent morality, was being pushed aside. Led by the Anti-Saloon League, the movement now focused on quelling the immorality of the lower classes; the impoverished needed saving from themselves. The moral suasion of Channing and Cushing was replaced by the fire-and-brimstone rhetoric of Dry preacher Billy Sunday, who was quoted saying that he had no interest in a God who did not smite.

Jacob Wirth, a model of respectability, pushed hard against Prohibition. In 1911, he helped found a small newspaper with the sole aim of crusading against a local push for banning liquor sales. And in 1914 and 1915, his name appeared proudly as distributor for Budweiser in a newspaper ad campaign run by Anheuser-Busch that sought to link beer drinking to American values of freedom. Large ads featuring images of the Statue of Liberty or the Founding Fathers declared that citizens had the right to drink. John Hancock himself would "have frowned upon any legislation which would restrict the natural rights of man and would have voted NO to prohibition enactments."

After World War I underscored the argument that the country needed grain for food, not spirits (and wasn't it suspicious how the German-Americans loved beer?), Congress passed the Eighteenth Amendment in 1918 and submitted it to the states for approval.

Up to the last minute, Wets pleaded their case. On January 14, 1919, an ad in the *Boston Globe* used the ultimate scare tactic: "Will Bolshevism Come with National Prohibition?" asked the Association Opposed to National Prohibition. National Prohibition "was the most drastic assault upon personal freedom ever contemplated under a republican form of government—[and] will be the best excuse that can be offered to stir up strike among the people. If you will give it one moment's serious thought, you will realize this is so."

Perhaps many did give the issue serious thought. But not even the fear of the Red Menace could stop the Dry Tide. On January 16, 1919, the thirty-sixth state ratified the Eighteenth Amendment; dry advocates in Boston rang out church bells in celebration. The Volstead Act, which provided terms for Prohibition enforcement, was passed on October 28, 1919. On January 16, 1920, Boston, like the rest of the nation, went officially dry. John Barleycorn was dead. Sort of.

GIN RICKEY

Cube of ice
Juice of ½ or whole lime
2 ounces dry gin

Combine ingredients. Fill with soda water
and serve with a small bar spoon. Serve in
a highball glass. Garnish with a slice of lime.

✳

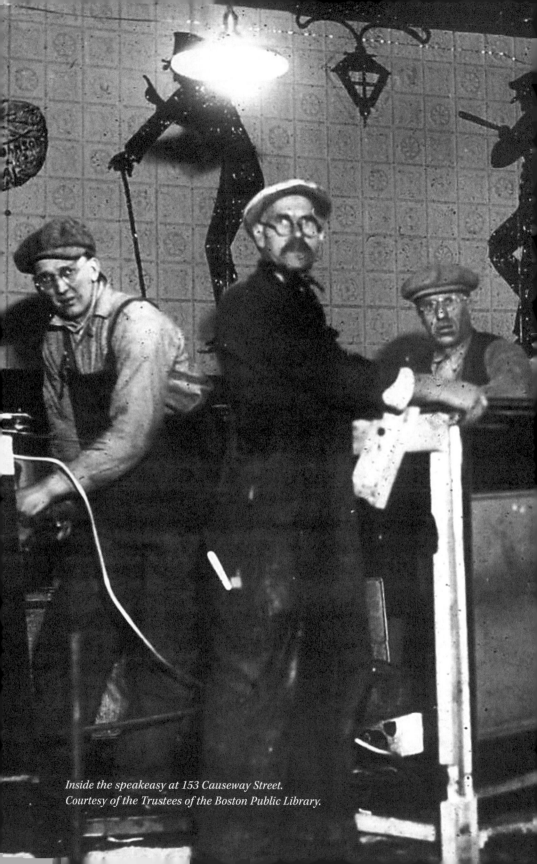

PROHIBITION, PART II: INSIDE THE SPEAKEASY

The year was 1932. Fresh from a stint at the Charles Street jail, Butsy O'Reilly and his pals Matty and Knobby were off to wet their whistle. At Dinty's, a place they knew in South Boston, they pressed the hidden buzzer and after being recognized, were admitted to the inner sanctum of the speakeasy.

"Well, well," exclaimed Dinty cheerily. "If it ain't Butsy O'Reilly! Believe me Butsy, it's a pleasure to see you around again."

"Thank you, Dinty, and I assure you, it's a treat to see you again."

"I'm glad of that," said Dinty. "And now if you guys will step up to the bar, I'll give you the best drink in the joint. I have some real good scotch that I was saving for just such an occasion. It's the real McCoy, too. A friend of mine who had it since before Prohibition gave it to me. I damn near lost it about an hour ago when the raiding squad paid me a visit. But luckily, they missed it."

"Did they find anything?" asked Butsy.

"No, it was the in-town squad, and I had been tipped off they were coming. But it never dawned on me to get rid of the bottle of scotch. For a minute or two while they were fooling around near the wall panel where it was hid, I felt ill. Not only would I have lost a good bottle of booze, but I would have got pinched along with it."

"As long as they didn't, we had better drink it now," said Butsy, "and there'll be no chance of losing it later."

"O.K.," said Dinty, setting the bottle on the bar. "Don't let your pee get hot. Would you like a chaser with it?"

"A chaser?" said Butsy, disdainfully. "And spoil the taste of the scotch?"

The boys settled in with their drinks with a warm glow of fellowship and no little satisfaction that Prohibition law had been thwarted once again.

—Edited excerpt from an unpublished novel by Thomas "Sandy" Richardson, who was convicted for the 1950 Brink's robbery in Boston, based on his life growing up in South Boston

Twenty-seven-year old Benjamin Krasoff has a dubious Boston distinction. According to the *Boston Globe*, he was the first person in Boston to be arrested under the new Prohibition law. On January 17, 1920, police nabbed him in a store in Dorchester and seized a number of bottles of "jakey," possibly a reference to Jamaica Ginger. We know nothing about Krasoff's fate, but he was just one lawbreaker of a multitude to follow. Meanwhile, hotel and restaurants struggled to adjust to serving dry meals. Bar owners were in despair; nothing with more than one half of one percent alcohol could be served. Only a few stragglers bellied up for cider or ginger flip. Desperate owners tried everything: hot dogs, sandwiches, pig's feet, anything to keep customers, but most intended to shut down as soon as their leases expired.

Others, however, looked for ways to slack the thirst of customers below the radar of Prohibition agents.

The origin of the word "speakeasy" (like the word "cocktail") has various legends, but most seem to agree that it predates Prohibition by about three decades. Whatever the origin, it wasn't long before places to buy an illegal drink were emerging in Boston. Boston's speakeasies were not exactly the stuff of Hollywood, and today's hip, so-called speakeasies bear about as much resemblance to real speakeasies as the real Bonnie and Clyde do to stars Faye Dunaway and Warren Beatty. In October 1927, the *Boston Globe* published an insider's description purportedly written by Aubrey Winsmith, an English visitor who had offered his write-up to the *Globe*. Whether Winsmith existed or was the *nom de plume* for a reporter who didn't want to write openly about breaking the law is unknown. Still, Winsmith made acute observations; he visited four widely different drinking places and gamely recorded his observations.

Guided by a streetwise Boston friend, Winsmith was taken to the back of what appeared to be a magazine store. A door opened into a room with a twenty-foot bar, crowded with men. Gin was twenty-five cents apiece. "The liquor was painful to drink but economical," claimed Winsmith.

Another speakeasy was set in the parlor of a private dwelling; a maid served drinks at what resembled an afternoon tea party. "At first I thought that the daughter of the house had announced her engagement to the policeman on the beat, for he was there." Beer was fifty cents a bottle.

In a warehouse-based establishment, tipsy men regaled Winsmith with their life stories. When an "open-faced young man" began singing "My Wild Irish Rose," he was showered accordingly with quarters.

For the final act, Winsmith's guide brought him to the "aristocrat" of speakeasies, up several flights of stairs into a room festooned with handsome paintings and tables set with white clothes and plates of crackers and pretzels. Drinks were seventy-five cents.

As Winsmith's reporting shows, there was a range of speakeasies in Boston. In South Boston, for example, many Irish-Americans sold liquor from their homes to those who were known to the owners. But there were fancier joints, too. For a short time, the Club Garden on Causeway Street flourished as a hang out for social leaders, students, sports fans, and even politicians. Photos of the Club Garden near North Station showed a fully appointed bar with silhouettes of men with top hats painted on the wall. It was raided in 1932 following complaints made by a Beacon Hill man about his daughter's visits there. Police found French and Italian vermouth, Cointreau, Benedictine, crème de menthe, and Dubonnet, "all the fixin's of an old-fashioned bar," the reporter wistfully added. About $6,000 in booze was seized. Ironically, women had been banned from the club three weeks earlier because of worries about the impact of intoxicated women.

Raids were a matter of business for speakeasies or for businesses that sold liquor under the table. Less than a year after the passage of Prohibition, federal prohibition officers raided the venerable hotel Marliave, established in 1885 and which continues to operate as a restaurant today on Bosworth Street in downtown Boston. As several hundred onlookers watched, agents seized a gallon of moonshine and a few bottles of crème de menthe. Two days later on December 7, owner Isaac Bernstein pled not guilty to the charges of having two quarts of alcohol and twelve pints of bitters. On December 17, the charges were dropped, perhaps for a lack of evidence. No matter: in November 1923, the place was again raided and five gallons of mixed liquor and fifty-nine bottles of beer were seized.

It didn't take long for bootleggers and bartenders to get wise, devising elaborate procedures for warning clients of impending agents and for dumping liquor if and when the police appeared. The ever-observant Winsmith described one intricate system: "After we rang the bell, it took several minutes before the man arrived at the door, and locked it behind him, before he opened the door on a chain to look at us. This, said my friend, was almost certain protection against a raid. Between the two locked doors was a bell, which the barkeep could ring if officers appeared outside. At the bar, men receiving the signal could pour all the liquor down the sink before the raiders could break down the doors and get inside."

That raids were a cat-and-mouse game was clear to all involved. For example, in May 1930, Boston police raided 43 of 155 alleged speakeasies on Washington, Carver, Pine, Kingston, Tremont, and Shawmut streets, and in only a few places was liquor found and in no instance was there any large quantity. In fact, what the Boston Police Department mostly confiscated were doors, which would provide kindling wood for the station during the winter.

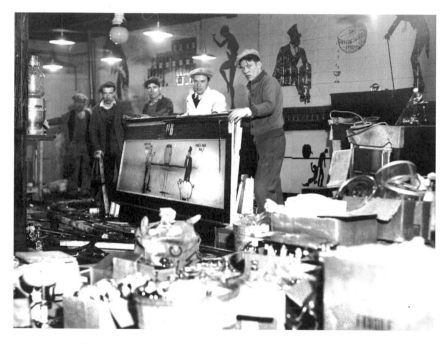

Dismantling a notorious speakeasy at 153 Causeway Street.
Courtesy of the Trustees of the Boston Public Library.

Drinkers also employed a good measure of Yankee ingenuity. When raiding police took a closer look at an ice chest full of milk, they discovered the bottles had been painted white while the liquid inside was far stronger. An innocent leg of lamb actually contained a hose; liquor poured out when the leg was held in a certain position. Booze was stashed in staircases, horse stalls, under rose bushes, and in tubs filled with soaking clothes. Complex hose systems were installed so that at the first sign of trouble, evidence could be washed away. One savvy police officer caught his crook by placing a container under a hose before he entered the house. The booze went right into the evidence bin. Officers found moonshine in teakettles sitting on stoves, and when an officer went to get a drink from a water cooler, he found it bubbling with gin.

The Faneuil Hall Club in the North End stashed its liquor in special sacks in another building across the alley; servers used long sticks with hooks at the end to reach through an open window and into that building to snag a sack. When raided, police couldn't find liquor, but they found the sticks and deduced the rest. When they searched the building across the alley, they found barrels of beer, fine whiskey, champagne, gin, and wine hidden in a secret room accessible only by a system of ropes and pulleys.

By the end of the decade, Boston had an estimated four thousand speakeasies (compared to an estimated one thousand licensed bars in the entire state in 1918), and fifteen thousand people engaged in illegally providing alcohol, not to mention those who frequented illegal bars around the city. This did not go unnoticed by Drys.

Delcevare King of Quincy, a wealthy banker and vice president of the Massachusetts Anti-Saloon League, believed fervently in the words of President Warren G. Harding: "Lawless drinking is a menace to the republic." But what to call these miscreants, lawbreakers, crooks, and villains who were making a mockery of the Noble Experiment?

King decided to sponsor a contest to come up with a word for the lawless drinker of illegal beverages. The prize was $200 and etymological glory. He laid down the rules: the winning word had to start with an "S" (since "S" carried a sting); it had to be of one or two syllables, and it could not just be an epithet for drinkers in general but for those who show reckless disregard for society. More than twenty-five thousand words were submitted; the winning entry was "Scofflaw," submitted by Henry Irving Dale of Andover and Kate L. Butler of Dorchester.

The *Boston Globe* had great fun in announcing the new word; an accompanying illustration spelled it "skofflaw" and showed it being used as a speakeasy password, a toast, and the call of a cuckoo clock, prompting the response, "It's time for another." Within a week, the famous Harry's New York Bar in Paris created a cocktail with rye and lemon and dubbed it "The Scofflaw." But King was so satisfied with the result, he immediately announced another contest for a one-hundred-word essay on the *proper* use of the word.

Not to be outdone, the *Harvard Advocate*, a Harvard campus paper, ran its own contest for an appropriate term for Drys, awarding, comparatively, a measly $25 to the winner: Spigot-bigot. Other entries included "pure tank," "jug buster," "fear-beer," "aquaduck," and "dryad." None of these words had the staying power of scofflaw, perhaps because Prohibition produced so many of them. Tellingly, documentary filmmaker Ken Burns, in his 2011 PBS series on Prohibition, called part two "A Nation of Scofflaws."

Likewise, Boston became a city of scofflaws. Bootleg liquor was available everywhere. The mayor of Boston, England, an honored guest in Boston, Massachusetts in 1930 for the city's three-hundredth anniversary, was quoted as saying he was astonished at the liquor laws in the state, which had enriched the bootlegger and rum-runner instead of the government. "You can swim in liquor there," the English mayor said. "You can drown yourself in it. They even offered to bring a load of it to my hotel in five minutes." Liquor even found its way in the jury room in the first trial of famed con artist Charles Ponzi in 1923, which found him innocent of larceny and conspiracy.

A wreath graces the door of a shuttered speakeasy.
Courtesy of the Trustees of the Boston Public Library.

"Judging from the breath of the men who drank it, it was horrible stuff," one juror said.

Much of the alcohol found in Boston at this time was vile: a good portion of it was made from denatured alcohol diverted from commercial uses, such as paint thinner. "Home brew," or "bathtub gin," was sometimes colored and sold as rye. Small distilleries outside Boston also made hooch from corn sugar, which was brought into the city by automobile. Better-quality spirits were smuggled in from Europe and the Caribbean and brought in by small boats off the coast of Cape Cod, Cape Ann, or near New Bedford. Even today many Bostonians will claim—often proudly—that some long lost relative smuggled liquor back in the 1920s. Of course, Boston's most famous *reputed* bootlegger is Joseph Kennedy, the son of barkeeper P.J. Kennedy and the father of future president John F. Kennedy. Joe Kennedy's involvement in bootlegging has long been accepted as fact in Boston, but the extent (and even if he was involved at all) has also been hotly disputed. The Kennedy patriarch was in the liquor importing business, but primarily after 1933, when it was legal. In his extensive book on Prohibition, *Last Call*, Daniel Okrent finds no decisive evidence that Kennedy made his fortune illegally smuggling in liquor, adding, "Joe Kennedy didn't have to be a bootlegger. After all, nearly everyone else was." Including a legendary gangster who emerged from obscurity to be the king of Boston's underworld.

THE SCOFFLAW

(Invented at Harry's Bar in Paris in 1924.)

1 ½ ounces rye
1 ounce dry vermouth
¾ ounce fresh lemon juice
¾ ounce real pomegranate grenadine

Shake in an iced cocktail shaker, and strain
into a cocktail glass.

Garnish with a lemon twist.

*At the scene of the Charles "King" Solomon murder
outside the Cotton Club in the South End.
Courtesy of the Trustees of the Boston Public Library.*

PROHIBITION, PART III:
GANGSTERS AND
DO-GOODERS

Every man who ever bought a pint from his bag-toting bootlegger contributed to Charlie Solomon's grotesque throne.

—*Boston Post,* January 29, 1933

In the wee hours of January 24, 1933, he strolled into the Cotton Club, a South End nightclub on Tremont Street catering to Boston's African-American community. On his arm were two lovely girls, blonde and brunette. His skillfully tailored suit fit him like a glove, his hair was slicked back and shining. His smile revealed rows of gleaming teeth, even while his eyes stayed distant, even cold. Both staff and customers greeted him warmly as he and his party sat down at a table, soon to be joined by another friend. As the jazz band played, the party drank, ate fried chicken, and laughed. The clock struck 4 am when another customer, a deputy sheriff, could not come up with the cash to pay his bill; the deputy approached, asking him to guarantee his check. It was signed "C.S." with a flourish and the waiter accepted it without question. A diamond ring twinkled from his hand, and a diamond watch and chain peeked from his jacket pocket. He paid his check by peeling off bills from a fold of about $4,600.

Charles Solomon, the man known as "King Solomon" and "Boston Charlie," was at the height of his power. From humble beginnings as the child of immigrants growing up on the docks in Salem to a career as a nightlife impresario, he had power, wealth, and notoriety to spare. His real business was talked about in whispers, even if his holdings had in recent years expanded to theaters, hotels, loan companies, real estate, and even a beauty shop for one of his paramours. Despite a long rap sheet and a recent federal indictment accusing him of being the brains behind a major rum-running ring, he was relaxed and confident. The potentially devastating news—a possible repeal of Prohibition—did not concern him at all. He was well-invested in legitimate businesses and could count politicians and other "respectable" citizens among his friends. No one dare touch him, neither those in authority, nor those outside the law.

Until that night, when an impulsive move by guys Solomon called "dirty rats" brought down the Capone of Boston.

Much of the life of Charles Solomon remains murky. He is mostly unknown today and if recalled at all, it is usually for his brief ownership of the Cocoanut Grove nightclub some years before a horrific fire killed nearly five hundred people there. Even Solomon's birth date is vague; he was born in either 1884 or 1886, possibly in Russia (one record indicates his parents came from Syria) to Jewish parents and was raised with three brothers on Derby Street in Salem, Massachusetts. Conflicting newspaper accounts say he first worked at a lunch cart and as a short-order cook. His skill on the dance floor won him the nickname

"Flyboots Charlie," although another account said he was known as "Sly Boots Charlie." He would later become a bondsman and developed a reputation as a "monster fence" for stolen goods. Just how much Solomon was shaped by the common anti-Jewish prejudice of the day, which prevented many Jews from full acceptance into American society, can't be determined. But by all accounts, Solomon was highly intelligent, charming, reserved, and ruthless.

Beginning about 1912, Charles Solomon started racking up a lengthy rap sheet. Charges against him included breaking and entering, receiving stolen goods, and prostitution-related offenses. He was soon involved with the narcotics trade—morphine and cocaine—and beat a serious charge of drug dealing in 1922 when a witness mysteriously changed her testimony. At the trial, when asked if he was the "dope king" of Boston, he took great offense. The "king" moniker stuck. He had another nickname, however, "False Front," so given because his genial charming exterior hid a hardened criminal.

Solomon ended up in prison after he was convicted for subordination of perjury for tampering with the witness at his 1922 narcotics trial. (He is alleged to have offered the witness $3,000 with the order to say, "You ain't sure it's him.") Sentenced to five years of hard labor in federal prison, he was released on a technicality after serving thirteen months. In 1924, he was charged with involvement in a $1.5 million mail fraud scheme in Los Angeles, although he insisted to reporters, "I have never been in Los Angeles in my life." The charges were later dismissed.

Dope turned to be less lucrative than dealing in a substance that used to be legal. Solomon, at some point, went into the bootlegging business. His role was primarily that of a financier, in term of arranging for payoff to ships bringing in alcohol from Europe, Canada, and the Caribbean. By most accounts he was good at what he did. "He had the brains and knew how to use them," said the *Boston Daily Record*. Along with Meyer Lansky, Dutch Schultz, Bugsy Siegel, Longy Zwillman, and Lepke Buchalter, Solomon was counted among the reputed Jewish Big Six of the East Coast, and he is said to have attended the Atlantic City Conference of organized crime in 1930, which aimed to settle beefs and divvy up profits. The depths of his involvement will never be known— this was a business without records, spreadsheets, or annual reports— but Solomon was soon rolling in loot and beginning to branch out, particularly into the entertainment businesses.

While no actual homicide was ever laid at the King's feet, it was common knowledge that he wasn't a person to be crossed. Austen Lake, a Boston tabloid reporter who wrote about Solomon in colorful detail (albeit with a shortage of actual facts), contended that while murder was not his "dish," Solomon "mingled and co-operated with the Big Shot mobsters of New York who, if they did not pull any triggers or swing any ice picks, had murder no less in their hearts." Solomon had, Lake insisted, ties with Murder Inc., the outfit that carried out hits for Jewish and Italian mobsters in New York from the 1920s to 1940s. When reporters once pressed Solomon's lawyer, Barney Welansky, about Solomon's criminal ties, Welansky would only say, "You knew him. What else can I tell you?"

In 1931, Solomon bought the swank Cocoanut Grove nightclub, which had been opened with a flourish in fall of 1927 by entertainer Mickey Alpert and musician Jacques Renard. Here, he hobnobbed with vaudeville stars, such as Sally Rand and the saucy Texas Guinan, who called him "old Rubber Lips." He didn't like publicity, and yet he liked the limelight. Indeed, Solomon, often dressed in a tuxedo or a white dinner jacket, was known to thousands of Bostonians as a suave nightclub owner—an entertainment czar who mingled with his clients. By the early 1930s, Solomon's history as a mob boss played second fiddle to his role as an entertainment czar.

Photos of him as a young man show a strong-featured fellow with large eyes, thick lips, and dark complexion, though in later years his lips appear strangely thinner. The King was known for being vain about his appearance. He was married twice, divorced once. He became estranged from his wife Bertha "Billie" Solomon and was seen mostly in the company of the glamorous Dorothy England, who operated the beauty parlor purchased for her.

No matter the genial appearance Solomon presented to the fawning crowds, he was not someone to disagree with. Angelo Lippi, who had been the popular maitre d' of the Cocoanut Grove when it first opened, described getting a call from the King after he bought the club, asking him to return to the nightclub from Hotel Touraine. "Of course I knew who Solomon was and his connections," Lippi recalled. He demurred and when asked about his salary, Lippi said he received $100 a week in his current position. Solomon just said, "You're hired, and you're coming to work for $100 a week." When Lippi picked up his first check, it was made out for $75. Furthermore, Lippi's name was used when the club applied for its licenses. In the end, he only made $35 a week and yet on paper he was the president and treasurer of the Cocoanut Grove Corporation. He dutifully signed checks for entertainers, handed to him by the club's bookkeeper, Rose Gnecco Ponzi, the wife of jailed pyramid scheme mastermind Charles Ponzi. Often, Lippi recalled, the payroll for entertainment topped $2,500 per week. Paradoxically enough, the Cocoanut Grove reportedly was never used as a speakeasy, unlike other clubs in the area; the King did not want to mix business and pleasure.

The King's empire eventually included interests in amusement companies, a gas company, a loan company, and restaurants and hotels in both Boston and New York City. He once bragged he was worth $10 million. Capone may have had a mob, but Solomon had a well-oiled machine. As a reporter noted: "The fact that newspapers outside Boston didn't know of Solomon until just before his death shows the quiet efficiency of his machine as compared to the noisy, shooting mob of Capone in Chicago at the same time." Given his varied investments, Solomon could have gone into a quiet retirement, but he couldn't quite bring himself to give up either the guns or the glamour. "I can't give it up," he reportedly told a friend. "It means everything to me. I've had enough of the hard and the rotten and miserable. I was always a bum to nice people. Now, when I put on those evening clothes and step through the door of the Cocoanut Grove, I'm a gentleman. I'm not a heel, you understand, I'm their host."

By January 3, 1933, however, Solomon's rule was drawing to a close. He and three others were named in an indictment by a federal grand jury in New York City on charges of operating a massive liquor-smuggling operation for the previous three years. According to the indictment, ships carrying liquor from Canada and Europe brought booze into New Jersey, guided by illicit radio stations along the Atlantic Coast. The weekly gross was said to be $1.25 million and Solomon was said to be one of the men in charge. Warned to keep out of the public eye, Solomon merely laughed and went about his business. He left a residence he kept at the Hotel Belvedere in New York and headed back to Boston where he told reporters that the charges were a result of a whisper campaign by politicians and enemies; he would have little difficulty in proving his innocence. "He ought to know, for if anybody ever knew the value of political ties, he was the one," the *Record* said.

The evening before he was due in federal court, he appeared, as was his habit, at the Cocoanut Grove for the evening, where he wined and

dined a pair of pretty young dancers, Claire White and Helen Ethridge—
he was apparently on the outs with his mistress, Dorothy England. At
about 3:30 am to keep the party going, Solomon and the girls grabbed
a cab to the Cotton Club, located on Tremont Street in the South End.
(Solomon may have even owned a piece of the club with impresario
Tommy Maren.)

At the Cotton Club, the party continued. When Solomon left his table to go to the bathroom, he was followed by a group of men who had
been drinking sullenly at a nearby table. Witnesses reported hearing an
argument, and then shots rang out. The men fled, and Solomon stag-
gered out, hit in the chest, abdomen, and neck. "The dirty rats got me,"
he hissed before being rushed to the hospital, where he died. He was
found to be missing his $4,600 roll of money, and an attempt had been
made to pull off his diamond ring.

*Charles "King" Solomon (left) with bandleader Joe Solomon, his frequent
companion Dorothy "Dot" England, and club maître d' Teddy Roy at the
Cocoanut Grove. Courtesy of the Trustees of the Boston Public Library.*

Many now feared a full-scale gang war would break out. "I believe Boston Charlie was put on the spot to seal his lips," said Assistant U.S. Attorney Leonard Greenstone. But it became likely that the perpetrators had acted on impulse, perhaps angry that Solomon had cut them out of the take for a recent robbery in a nearby town. For starters, they had checked their coats earlier in the evening, not a smart move when planning a hit.

Mourning the death of Charles "King" Solomon.
Courtesy of the Trustees of the Boston Public Library.

Solomon was buried on Thursday, January 26. Hundreds gathered at his grave, and thousands gathered outside his residence on Fuller Street in Brookline and along the street of his funeral procession to the Hand-in-Hand Cemetery in West Roxbury. Mounds of flowers were laid on his grave, and the morbidly curious snatched a few as souvenirs. Attending the funeral were mobsters Phil Buccola and David "Beano" Breen, as well as prominent attorney Herbert Callahan and Cotton Club owner Tommy Maren. White and Ethridge sobbed at the grave. Dorothy England did not attend. Solomon's sorrowful brother called him a big overgrown baby, as gentle as a kitten, and said he had last Christmas given away eight hundred baskets of food to the poor as well as thousands of dollars in gifts to friends.

Dozen of Boston's gangsters were picked up and questioned about the crime; three were eventually convicted in connection with the murder. Despite the millions he had allegedly amassed, Solomon's estate was later valued at only a few hundred dollars. The Cocoanut Grove passed to his lawyer, Barney Welanksy, who turned it into a profitable business. Bertha Solomon married a dentist. In March 1933, Alexander Lillien of New Jersey, who had been indicted with Solomon on the rum-running charges, was found with three bullets in the head. Boston gradually forgot about the man who once was called the King.

Solomon did not bring crime to Boston. Even without Prohibition, he was a criminal, albeit a wealthy one. Nor was he the only bootlegger; the Gustin Gang of South Boston and the Lombardo Gang in the North End were also in the bootlegging business with murder and mayhem following in their wake.

King Solomon was the most colorful and the most paradoxical of the bunch. Barely a year after his death, Prohibition was repealed. The King was dead. Long live the King.

Apart from sharing the same initials, Cora Frances Stoddard had almost nothing in common with Charles Solomon. But she, too, played an unusual, if ambiguous role in Boston's drinking life. Like many women of her day, whose true spirit was often tailored to societal dictates, Stoddard remains elusive. Her devotion to Prohibition and temperance—from a modern viewpoint—seems both quaint and misplaced. But Stoddard's life deserves a fresh look. Well-educated, fair-minded, and a meticulous researcher, she took one of the few political paths permissible for a woman of her class, that is, the temperance movement. Nothing in her writing suggests she was an ardent suffragette, but she pursued a career, forgoing a traditional family life. She suffered from ill health much of her life and ended up confined to a wheelchair due to crippling arthritis, but she stayed active and true to her vision to the end of her life. No matter how the modern reader may disagree with her opinions on drink, we have to admit that she attempted to prove her case with logic and facts. And, difficult as it is to admit in a book exploring (and celebrating) Boston's drinking history, in many ways she was right.

Stoddard was born in 1872 in Irvington, Nebraska, into a prominent New England family that could trace its roots back to John Stoddard, who was granted land in New England in 1638. Her family eventually moved back to New England.

Stoddard was a brilliant student at Wellesley College where she graduated in 1896; friends describe her as poised, an excellent writer, and passionate about social causes. Both parents were "constantly waging war on the saloon"—her father as a constable and her mother as a WCTU leader—and Cora took up their cause. In 1899, she became the private secretary to Mary Hanchett Hunt, the superintendent of the Women's Christian Temperance Union's Scientific Temperance Instruction arm.

When Hunt died in 1906, Stoddard took over as executive secretary of the Boston-based Scientific Temperance Federation and spent the next thirty years at its helm. She was ambitious; she wanted the federation to do "large and important work," as a friend said, and Stoddard set out to prove beyond a doubt the harmful effect of alcohol on health, welfare, and social good. Unlike Hunt, who was given to hyperbole, Stoddard wanted the research of the federation to "stand the most scrutinizing tests." She considered herself foremost a scientist; "She did not act quickly," a friend recalled. "She took time to view the question from all sides, and her conclusions were accepted without question." The portrait that emerges is quite unlike the popular view of temperance advocates, usually the dour-faced ladies with signs that read: "Lips that touch liquor shall not touch ours." A photo of Stoddard shows an attractive woman with gentle eyes and a hint of a smile. Stoddard was soon considered among the leaders of the Prohibition movement, and after the passage of the Eighteenth Amendment she joined other luminaries who gathered to celebrate in Washington, D.C.

But it was only after Prohibition was passed that Stoddard did her "large and important" work. Now she would have a chance to prove what so many Dry advocates claimed: that a ban on alcohol would decrease child abuse, mortality rates, hospitalization rates, and crime, in short, that it would usher in a period of better conditions for all. Many of Stoddard's research notes—which have been preserved in a massive collection of temperance papers—attest to her devotion to gathering actual evidence and subjecting it to sober (so to speak) analysis.

Meticulously, she gathered figures: on the number of arrests for drunkenness, hospitalization rates, crime rates, delinquency, and mental health. Her notes, painstakingly jotted down, reveal a woman devoted to her work, one who wrote letters, devised questionnaires, clipped articles, and produced a steady stream of articles.

Even just two years after Prohibition went into effect, Stoddard (perhaps not shockingly) concluded there had been a marked decrease in drunkenness, offenses against the public, abuse cases against children—even mortality rates. There was a rise in savings accounts as people banked the money that previously went to pay the bar tab. Her crowning achievement was her massive study "Fifteen Years of the Drink Question in Massachusetts" in which she compared seven consecutive years of data before Prohibition to seven years afterwards.

Her writing is generally free of moralistic cant—she was trying to prove what any social service worker will say today: that alcohol abuse plays a role in domestic violence, crimes, personal injury, and ill health. Today, Stoddard might be a member of Mothers Against Drunk Driving, an anti-smoking activist, a social worker, a drug counselor, or a public-health researcher in a major university.

Even if Stoddard's data inevitably showed that alcohol was harmful, she had to realize by the late 1920s that the bright promise of Prohibition was dimming. The graphs she created of rates of drunkenness, crimes, and alcohol-related insanity had to make that clear to her. After a precipitous drop in 1921, the rates had started to creep up. By the mid-1920s, even ardent Drys had to admit alcohol was flowing in Boston and throughout the nation. Whatever health benefit accrued to a sober population was being wiped away by continued drinking, often of wood alcohol, Jamaica Ginger, or other unreliable sources in unregulated conditions.

Something else was changing. The link between the women's suffrage and temperance movements started to fray. By the 1930s, a substantial number of women had turned against the Eighteenth

Amendment. In 1932, Women's Organization for National Prohibition Reform took up the argument that Prohibition had increased alcohol consumption, crime rates had gone up, and personal liberties had been weakened. The leaders charged that the government was losing millions of dollars in potential taxes while forcing it to spend millions of dollars on enforcement. White-frocked women marched in New York with signs declaring, "We Want Beer."

Stoddard carried on. She was, however, on the losing end of the debate and a muckraker from Minnesota was about to tip the balance.

Walter W. Liggett was the kind of reporter who lived by the code, "afflict the comfortable and comfort the afflicted." Born on Valentine's Day in 1886, he became a newspaperman in 1905 and worked at a variety of publications before turning to freelance investigative reporting. A crusader, as well as a journalist, and a Bohemian of sorts (he once lived in an artist colony in Provincetown), he was among those seeking justice for two Italians from Plymouth, Massachusetts, accused of murder: Bartolomeo Vanzetti and Nicola Sacco. Soon he was writing for *Plain Talk* magazine, a monthly opinion journal founded in 1927 by G. D. Eaton. *Plain Talk* was among the many high-minded magazines launched in the 1920s; today the *New Yorker*, founded in 1925, is one of the remaining survivors. Liggett's primary target was the lawlessness and hypocrisy fostered by the Eighteenth Amendment. From September 1929 to August 1930, Liggett crisscrossed the country to research the impact of Prohibition. He spent nearly a month in Boston.

The article "Bawdy Boston" appeared in the January 1930 issue of *Plain Talk*. It caused a sensation. "Bootlegging is the largest and best paying racket in Boston at the present time," Liggett declared. He went on:

To give some idea of the graft involved it merely need be mentioned that now, after ten years of so-called Prohibition, the people of Boston are spending at least $60,000,000 a year for illicit hooch. There are at least 4,000 places in Greater Boston where booze is sold, and approximately 15,000 persons are more or less intermittently engaged in dispensing alcoholic liquor. At least 5,000 of this number are professional bootleggers with no other occupation, the most successful of whom are affiliated with a well-organized ring which operates speakeasies in every part of Boston...Boston is literally honeycombed with speakeasies. There hardly is a building in town that does not contain at least one office where bottle liquor may be had. Most of these speakeasies are camouflaged as brokers' offices, wool dealers or real-estate firms...Stylishly dressed women frequently purchased bottled booze over the counter while policemen lazily lounged in the front door.

Liggett decried the way that Charles "King" Solomon, the "head of the dope racket," managed to evade capture and "is still living in affluence in Boston, a prominent figure in the night life of the underworld." But Liggett was not attacking the proliferation of booze, rather the hypocrisy of state officials, from the police to the mayor, who allowed lawlessness to flourish or who directly profited from it. With relish, he wrote: "Many of the Cape-Codders who assisted the rum-runners are the direct descendants of the Pilgrim Fathers. There is a certain grim humor in tracing the operations of a statute which makes lawbreakers of these people."

Liggett's charges left politicians sputtering with shock. Efforts were made to ban the issue of *Plain Talk* in which "Bawdy Boston" ran, but it reportedly sold out in a day. State and city officials brushed off Liggett's contention as a mere rehashing of newspaper headlines. "There is nothing in it that is new," sniffed U.S. District Attorney Frederick Tarr. But Liggett's analysis also stung officials into action. Tarr convened a grand jury and called Liggett in to testify. The grand jury ended on February 19, 1930, with no indictments; it merely released a feeble statement that "an investigation by the proper tribunal of the activities by some of the Boston police departments should be made."

Liggett went on to write other exposés for *Plain Talk* in articles such as "Holy Hypocritical Kansas," "Georgia: Godly but Guzzling," "Michigan: Soused and Serene," and "Whoopee in Oklahoma." Called to testify before the U.S. Congress, he repeated his charges about Boston and other cities. When Liggett said, "If we have ten more years of Prohibition, the nation will be ruled by gangsters, underworld rats, and crooked politicians," the room erupted into applause.

Not even the tenacious Liggett could name all the Boston politicians, police, and officials tangled up with the liquor racket. Publishing the names in the era's phone book would probably be the only way to cover them all. But one man stands out for his sheer audacity and brazenness.

Oliver Garrett cut a dashing figure as head of the city's liquor squad. A veteran of World War I, he joined the Boston Police Department in 1919 (three months after a massive police strike) and was assigned to the Charlestown division. Within a few years he was promoted to head of the vice squad, often leading raids himself. In nine years, his squad had made seventeen thousand arrests, and more than twenty-five thousand raids. "No man was more feared by bootleggers than Garrett," claimed an article in the *Boston Globe*. Garrett's heroics were the stuff of Hollywood, leading raids himself, jumping from roof to roof, leaping across alleyways, and lowering himself through skylights. In 1924, his

Boston Police Liquor Squad led by Oliver Garrett (second from right)
dressed up in evening clothes for visits to Boston hotels on New Year's Eve.
Courtesy of the Trustees of the Boston Public Library.

hand was seriously injured while grabbing a glass pitcher containing liquor during a raid. In 1927, he suffered a broken nose and was knocked unconscious when he jumped in to break up a fight in the South End. In 1928, Chinese gangs, angered when he broke up an opium-smoking den, put a price on his life, which he defied. But within the year, seemingly out of the blue, he was demoted and kicked back to being an ordinary police officer.

In "Bawdy Boston," Liggett had tagged Garrett as a "million dollar cop" who, with no visible income beyond his $40-a-week salary, had a farm, a racing stable, a Cadillac, a Marmon, a Chrysler, and a wardrobe of $150 tailored suits. "It is the belief of Boston newspaper reporters that Garrett was 'bagman' for certain higher-ups who finally got rid of him because they were not satisfied with their percentage of the split," Liggett reported.

Garrett's hubris was undimmed by allegations he was on the take. Claiming he had been injured in a car accident on the job, he quit and applied for his pension. Police Commissioner Herbert Wilson granted it, setting off a storm of anger and a series of hearings. A different portrait of the heroic Garrett emerged. John F. Sullivan of the Hotel Ritz testified that Garrett had forced him to hire a friend named Lillian Hatch as a hatcheck girl in the hotel. Hatch then accepted payoffs for Garrett. In May 1930, Garrett was indicted on extortion charges. After two trials failed to convict him and facing a third, Garrett pled guilty and was sentenced to two years in the Deer Island prison.

It was not hard time. There were rumors he had his own speedboat to come and go, and he owned season tickets to the Red Sox. Upon his release in 1933, he tried a career as a master of ceremonies in nightclubs, but soon slipped from sight. Then in 1944, Garrett sued the city for pension payments dating back to 1930. Finally in 1952, he received a judgment for $19,492, but settled for $4,567 and agreed never to again sue the city.

Not every cop in Boston could be bought.

On Valentine's Day in 1940, a huge blizzard blanketed Boston, but James Sheehan—a Boston cop, family man, and devout Catholic—was determined to make it to Mass. He piled his wife and sons in the car and the family inched along the road. On the way, he saw two fellow officers shoveling out a car. He stopped, ready to congratulate them on their act of kindness, when he recognized the owner of the car—it belonged to a man Sheehan knew to be a racketeer. Sheehan's son William was sitting in the car and saw his father's anger that two of his fellow officers could be so compromised. Decades later he recalled the incident and was reminded of his father's words: "Once you take their first dollar, they own you."

A native of South Boston, James Sheehan joined the police force in 1920 after a stint as a fireman and developed a reputation as a relentless investigator, winning the nickname "racket buster." But during the hearings over deposed vice squad leader William Garrett's shakedown of the Ritz, Sheehan was accused of being at the Ritz on March 3, 1928, and involved in the illegal activities that transpired there. Sheehan's story might have been different except for his careful record keeping. Sheehan was able to produce his memorandum book that showed he was on duty at the station that night. Even the implication of wrongdoing might have derailed a law enforcement career, but not in this case. Sheehan would later become head of the vice squad and have a distinguished law enforcement career; he organized the Boston Police's bureau of records, made innovations in fingerprints, and was one of the first to attend the new FBI school in Washington, D.C. He retired in 1952 and died two years later at age sixty of a heart attack. After the funeral colleagues told his son, "Your father could have been a multi-millionaire." A plaque to Sheehan hangs in Boston Police Headquarters, placed there in 2010 as part of the FBI's celebration of its seventy-fifth anniversary.

SIDECAR

1 ounce brandy

1 ounce Cointreau

1 ounce fresh lemon juice

Shake well with cracked ice and strain into a
chilled cocktail glass with a sugared rim.

Courtesy of the Trustees of the Boston Public Library.

PROHIBITION, PART IV: JOHN BARLEYCORN LIVES

The sad fate of Prohibition can be blamed on poor handling. Once on the throne, Prohibition began to spend millions like a drunken sailor. Hypocritically, he went to church on Sundays to keep the good opinion of his lady admirers. But on the other six days, he consorted with the dregs of the underworld. His intimate friends were so low that even the old champion, Barleycorn, would have nothing to do with him. His managers saw him kick women and children on the streets, bribe police, and make a joke of justice. But they still tried to sell him to the public as a noble experiment.

—Myles T. McSweeney, *Boston Daily Record*,
"New Champeen! John Barleycorn," December 6, 1933

On December 5, 1933, Boston welcomed back an old friend. "Hub Hails 'King Rum,'" was emblazoned across the front of the *Daily Record*. "Hub Revels as Liquor Flows, City Alive with Gay Throngs," the *Post* said. The newspapers carried front-page photos of Massachusetts Governor Joseph Ely, Senator David I. Walsh, and attorney Declan Corcoran sharing the first drink served legally at the Copley Plaza Hotel. Their choice? A martini.

"Hey John, what kept you," writer John Barry wondered in the *Boston Globe*, adding, "The bibulous, bottle-shaped old rake who was supposed to have been laid away for all eternity amidst joyful hallelujahs

Crowds celebrate Repeal on Boston streets.
Courtesy of the Trustees of the Boston Public Library.

from the left and mournful requiems from the right, fourteen years ago was only experimenting with death. He was doing a Rip Van Winkle in modern dress."

Repeal night was a not a time for fine dining but a time to gulp and gallop. Prices were low: twenty-five cents for a whiskey at most places, with cocktails from forty to seventy-five cents. Around the city, they sipped Manhattans, Orange Blossoms, gin fizzes, gin sours, rum cocktails, Old Fashioneds, Zazas, Presidentes, silver fizzes, Tom Collinses, rum rickeys, gin bucks, blended rye highballs, Dubonnet, champagne cocktails, and the famous Ward Eight. Many people came out just to watch other people drink. In the mad jubilation on the night of Repeal, customers thronged Jacob Wirth's. (Unfortunately, the establishment had not yet obtained a license and put up signs to that effect; they were still selling near beer.) No matter; the crowd celebrated as if they were putting back one-hundred proof spirits.

John Barleycorn was pretty battered by this time. Just a week earlier, Governor Ely had declared a "war to the finish" on speakeasies and illicit nightclubs, pledging, "Every speakeasy, unlicensed nightclub, and other illegal resorts will be driven from the city with a few days." But with Repeal pending—the nation was awaiting the last state to ratify the Eighteenth Amendment—the law was being openly flouted. On Thanksgiving eve, every club and speakeasy in the city was open. Police raided the Vanity Fair club on Newbury Street six times between 10 pm and 2:30 am. They never found evidence of alcohol. Patrons jeered as the police walked in again, looked around, and walked back out. When the blue coats left, the drinking recommenced.

A few days later, Ely, without an ounce of shame, posed with his martini cocktail for the cameras to mark the end of an era. Prohibition was over.

Newspaper photos of repeal night reveal a sea change in gender relations. Many of the photos of happy people drinking featured young women—hair coiffed, fingernails painted, lipstick bright—sipping their drinks, smiling directly into the camera without reservation. Whereas saloons had been male sanctuaries, speakeasies were often open to both men and women. "Prohibition sanctioned women to share liquor with men frankly, without surreptitiousness or shame," *The Hour: A Cocktail Manifesto* explained.

IN SPRING OF 2012, the author and friends set out to find a hip new bar in Union Square, Somerville. The Internet yielded the address, but that only led to a dark alley. We wandered up and down until we finally noticed a door under a single light. Opening the door, we could now hear voices and laughter down the corridor. We followed the sound and found ourselves in backbar. The password? "Do you have reservations?"

Like the speakeasies of old, new bars in Boston are showing off by hiding in plain sight. Places like Saloon in Davis Square, Somerville, and Brick & Mortar in Central Square, Cambridge, with their limited signage and "you have to know it to find it" sensibilities are courting a sense of intrigue, as if the drinks they offer are actually illicit, not just very expensive. Marliave, which was, indeed, raided during Prohibition, has a downstairs room, accessible through an outside door, that stands in as a "speakeasy." Gimmicky, perhaps. But fun just the same. It all proves that people tend to crave what they can't get and even if what they think they can't find is actually right before their eyes. And perfectly legal.

While some women did frequent Boston bars before Prohibition, they were often made welcome in speakeasies; by Repeal, seeing women in bars was quite commonplace. As one author puts it, "The old days when father spent his evenings at Cassidy's bar with the rest of the boys are gone, and probably gone forever; Cassidy may still be in business at the old stand and father may still go down there on evenings but since Prohibition, mother goes with him." From now on, public drinking was not a male only activity. To underscore the point, in 1934, the *Globe* sent out another female reporter to investigate women's drinking habits. She found that while women were drinking such concoctions as brandy milkshakes, Planter's Punch, Old Fashioneds, and martinis, they were not, it seemed, getting drunk. One bartender told reporter Shirley Mulliken, "You'd be surprised how many women order straight whiskey...They can take it without showing it, most of them. On the whole, I think women hold liquor a lot better than men." However at a "large and splendid bar" near the *Globe* building, a bartender told Mulliken about the last time he had to cut one young lady off. "Why that pert little thing gave me the prettiest punch on the jaw you ever saw. I was leaning over to tell her I was surprised at a lovely looking girl like her getting drunk when she up and gave me a good poke." The young lady was escorted from the premises.

There were, however, efforts to differentiate against the sexes. The Massachusetts legislature filed a bill to force tavern owners to sell to either men or women, but not both. And despite Repeal, Massachusetts drinking laws would become entangled in myriad ways. Illegal sales of liquor continued; speakeasies would only slowly die out as the city and state continues to wrestle with the issues of individual freedom and public good. Closing hours, zoning, food service, taxes, and so many other issues would convulse the state in the years to come. Underground after-hour bars continue to this day. Just as temperance advocates hoped that Prohibition would usher in a new era of good health, Wets now hoped Repeal would end the country's tilt into lawlessness. Neither hope came true.

Walter Liggett went on to edit *Plain Talk*, and when that folded, he continued to write exposés, including a major biography of Herbert Hoover and sensational reports about Minnesota's governor. In 1935, at age forty-nine, he was mowed down by machine gun fire before his wife and ten-year-old daughter outside his Minneapolis home. Gangster Isadore "Kid Cann" Blumenfeld was charged with the murder but never convicted. Liggett is still considered one of the country's great muckraking journalists, who paid with his life for his profession.

What Cora Frances Stoddard thought of the wild celebrations at Repeal, no one knows. She died three years later at age sixty-four, confined to a wheelchair by crippling arthritis. The entire summer 1936 edition of the *Scientific Temperance Journal* was devoted to her. In it, Delcevare King (the "scofflaw" contest creator) called her a saint. Activist Arthur J. Davis paid her a higher compliment: She was a scientist. "Her contribution to the temperance cause was infinitely greater because she was invariably guided by scientific facts, not emotion." It's a lesson worth considering in today's overwrought political discourse.

CHAMPAGNE COCKTAIL

In a champagne flute:

1 sugar cube
4 dashes of Angostura bitters

Fill with champagne.
Garnish with a lemon twist.

✳

Chorus line dancers from the 1940s. Courtesy of Ronald Arntz.

THE CONGA BELT: NIGHTCLUBS IN BOSTON

We didn't have television at the time. If you wanted to go celebrate, you went to a nightclub. You went to a place where you could dance and dine and be seen. It was glamour! It was wonderful! It was alive! You weren't in your dining room living vicariously through a screen. You were actually there. Nightclubs offered you an opportunity to get out of the doldrums into something exciting and something glamorous, and you dressed that way and you acted that way. You had corsages and you had champagne and you had five-course meals and maitre d's and cigarette girls and hatcheck girls and things of that sort.

—Edith Nussinow, daughter of bandleader Jacques Renard
Interview with author, January 2011

In early 2012, the lush lasses of the Boston chapter of the Ladies United for the Preservation of Endangered Cocktails pulled out the stops for a fundraiser, something called "The Snow Ball." The Boston chapter of LUPEC, a classic cocktail society "dedicated to breeding, raising, and releasing nearly extinct drinks into the wild" had been founded in February 2007 by bartender Misty Kalkofen and nine cocktail enthusiasts. Mixing eras, if not metaphors, LUPEC staged the Snow Ball in the downstairs lounge of Silvertone Bar & Grill in downtown Boston, and partygoers dressed accordingly. A silver disco ball sent sparkles rippling over the crowd; attendees received complimentary wrist corsages, boutonnieres, and hip flasks.

A makeshift photography studio allowed subjects to pose against a gauzy white backdrop with ivory columns. Happy couples, gay and straight, posed and nuzzled. One woman wore her prom dress complete with tiara; another showed off Japanese characters tattooed down her back. Men wore crisply tailored suits and ties, their dates in sleek cocktail dresses or equally crisp suits. Some sipped Manhattans. Others sampled drinks prepared for the occasion, including a potent tipple called "Heavy Petting Punch," which had Wild Turkey, Sailor Jerry, black tea, and sherry among the ingredients.

The soiree was a throwback to an era—but which one? A 1920s speakeasy? A 1940s nightclub? A 1950s prom night? A 1970s disco? Or was this an example of a twenty-first century mash-up, with styles and sensibilities shaken and stirred together like one of the multi-ingredient craft cocktails being poured at the bar? The scene was not precisely glamorous, but a send-up of glamour: "Mad Men" meets Joan Crawford meets Betty Boop meets "Barbarella." A businessman, in town from the West, wandered in and was astonished by the crowd. It was not at all what he expected of stodgy Boston.

Yet, once upon a time, Boston glittered and sparkled, and not in a self-mocking, retro way. Boston had nightclubs where chorus girls kicked for the ceiling, musicians did hot licks until dawn, and the wealthy, the wannabe wealthy, and the working class briefly forgot their cares with the sip of a drink and a turn on the dance floor. Boston dressed up like a dame on the town, ready to see and be seen.

Boston's nightclub era—if it can be called that—has almost been lost to history. Memories of once-hopping joints such as the Latin Quarter, the Mayfair, the Hi-Hat, and the Pioneer Club are fading, recalled only by certain age groups, neighborhood historical societies, or jazz history aficionados. The stories of these places, often associated with over-indulgence of appetites for drinking and other kinds of improper behavior, seldom appear in "official" histories. But that is why they were so loved; these venues were exotic and fanciful in their designs, and communicated an aura of the forbidden and the naughty. The main selling point may have been glamour, but the nightclub business was fed by alcohol—indeed, drinking kept it afloat. Lubricated by booze and bathed in tobacco smoke in ways that would flummox today's more health-conscious society, the nightclubs of Boston transported an entire population to another time and place for a healthy dose of escapist fantasy.

Boston isn't exactly known as the city that never sleeps or that toddlin' town, Chicago. Given its compact size, its Puritan heritage, its Watch and Ward Society, its working-class streets, and its Brahmin snobbery, Boston has always played second fiddle to New York. (Except in baseball, of course.) There are and have always been neighborhood bars galore in Boston, as well as student bars, rarified private clubs, dance joints, discos, and dives too numerous for any one book to chronicle. However, there was a time, from the mid-1920s through the 1940s, when the evening was ruled by the nightclub and supper club. In the city's Theater District and South End and the now-quiet neighborhood known as Bay Village, Boston's late-night drinking scene sparkled with a zest we can only picture in black-and-white, our impressions fixed by Hollywood films and old photographs. These were not speakeasies, although patrons often drank there from set ups (where glasses, ice, and mixers were served to patrons who supplied their own liquor) or hip flasks. They were not hole-in-the wall blind pigs, but showcases that (unlike the burlesque shows at the infamous Howard in Scollay Square) were designed for couples, family groups, lunching ladies, and even, at times, youngsters. Today, many of Boston's hip bars claim to be capturing a speakeasy atmosphere, but what they are really channeling is the spirit of the 1930s and 1940s nightclub.

The rock 'n' roll generation can barely remember the names of these relics of nightlife past; for all members of Generation X and Generation Next know, they could be written in hieroglyphics. For an older generation of Bostonians, however, these names conjure cherished memories, even if those memories are fading. The Latin Quarter. Club Mayfair. The Cocoanut Grove. The Brown Derby. Casa Manana. Fox & Hounds. Rio Casino. The Music Box at the Copley Square Hotel. The Terrace Room at Hotel Statler. Hotel Touraine. Lido Venice on Warrenton Street. The Roundup on Huntington Avenue. The Egyptian Room at the Hotel Brunswick. The Southland Club. A bit later, havens such as the Hi-Hat, the Savoy, Storyville, and Connolly's nurtured hot jazz, while members of the Rat Pack cooled their jets at Blinstrub's Village in South Boston.

Somewhat ironically, this era of sparkling and sizzling nightlife began during that great dry spell called Prohibition. In May 1940, George W. Clark of the *Boston Advertiser* described the birth of Boston's nightclub era with the cadence of a fairy tale:

> *Once upon a time there wasn't any Cocoanut Grove or Mayfair or Kitty Brando's or Latin Quarter, either for that matter, or Southland or Casa Manana...but there were a lot of speakeasies scattered about the town, masquerading as cigar stores, dairy lunches —even as coal offices and book shops. Then overnight it seems, night clubs blossomed where none had bloomed before and out of nothing came what we have come to call 'The Conga Belt'— that strange maze of twisted streets where the retail district ends and where, when darkness comes, neon signs create a counterfeit paradise of lovely girls, gay music, wine, and song.*

Prohibition could not stop the flow of liquor into Boston, and pious proponents like Billy Sunday or Wayne B. Wheeler couldn't stop the

Two sailors inside Casa Manana. From the author's collection.

fun either. Bostonians wanted a night on the town, even if liquor was forbidden or was smuggled in while waiters looked the other way. The first quasi-nightclub in the city might be considered the Brunswick Hotel, where, according to the *Boston Globe*, the city's first outdoor café was opened and where dancing was hosted in its dimly lit Egyptian Room as early as 1918, courtesy of Leo Riesman's orchestra. By 1929, dozens of venues had sprung up. On New Year's Eve, 1928, crowds flocked to see the shows at clubs like the Lido Venice, the City Club, University Club, and Cocoanut Grove. "All the little clubs scattered through the Back Bay and South End were crowded to the doors," the *Globe* reported on January 1, 1929.

Perhaps the most sumptuous of the bunch was a club launched in 1927 by two men with a vision for a South Seas watering hole in dry Boston: Milton Irving Alpert, known as Mickey Alpert, an ambitious furniture salesman who yearned to be a club impresario, and musician Jacques Renard.

Renard, born Jacob Joseph Staviski, was a classically trained musician who turned to popular music when early arthritis hurt his violin playing. He loved the sounds of the burgeoning jazz scene and created a band that matched that music with a lush violin backdrop, a melodious result with a popular commercial appeal. "He used the violin as the main instrument as Benny Goodman used the clarinet and Dorsey had the trombone," his daughter recalled. A French-sounding stage name—Jacques Renard—enhanced his class-act appeal. Portly and bespectacled, and a pioneer in live radio broadcasts, Renard moved easily through the ranks of the nation's top musicians. He was already an in-demand bandleader when he and Alpert took over a former garage and film repository on Piedmont Street, between Church Street and Broadway, a street now truncated by hotel development. With a design by the famed nightclub decorator Rueben Bodenhorn, they launched the Renard Cocoanut Grove, named for the headliner and the famous Los Angeles nightspot. Renard led the Cocoanut Grove Victor Recording Orchestra while Mickey Alpert, "the boy impresario," brought "a collection of real trouble makers" for entertainment.

Problems emerged almost immediately after the club's launch in October 1927. The club's owners were hard-pressed to make a profit without selling alcohol, even though Renard adamantly opposed it. But other forces were at work. Edith Nussinow, Renard's daughter, recalls the pressure put on her father by people he never identified. "They took my mother for a proverbial ride. Put her in the back seat of a Roadster and covered her up with a blanket and took her for a ride to Revere Beach. She said there were machine guns under the sheet with her." She was safely returned with the order that her husband fall in line and improve the club's bottom line with liquor sales.

The anxiety was too much for Renard, and Alpert bought him out. Alpert later sold the club for a mere $10,000 to Charles "King" Solomon. After Solomon's murder at the Cotton Club, his lawyer, Barney Welansky, took over the Grove, expanded it, and turned it into a profitable business, particularly after Prohibition was repealed in 1933.

Renard didn't go far—just up the street to a new venture: the Renard Mayfair Club at 54 Broadway. The Mayfair was a smaller club, and Renard eventually left for California to work with singer and performer Eddie Cantor, and he later moved to New York to work with comedian Joe Penner. The Mayfair continued to prosper although it changed owners and names a number of times. Renard would eventually return to Boston where he became a mainstay at the Bradford Hotel roof and as a society bandleader.

By the mid-1930s, it became evident that vaudeville was losing its popularity. Observing this, a young English-born talent agent, Lou Walters, shrewdly began focusing on producing and promoting nightclub acts more refined, and yet often more risqué, than aging comedians or specialty acts. Walters made a name for himself when he staged a show with a female impersonator and a chorus of "debutantes"—actually trained dancers—at the Club Lido Venice on Warrenton Street. He even got the notorious Evelyn Nesbitt to appear. However, it was the gamble he took in 1937 that would change nightclub history in Boston and beyond.

There was a time in Boston when famed newscaster Barbara Walters was referred to as Lou Walters's little girl. That was soon after Walters took over the former Karnak Club on Winchester Street near Park Square and built a new kind of nightclub. His daughter recalls in her memoir:

Boston had its share of nightclubs already. What Boston did not have was an inexpensive nightclub that served a full dinner for under ten dollars and was naughty enough for grownups but tame enough for families. My father toyed at first with using the Congo as a theme, with lions and tigers painted on the wall and a chorus line of pretend native dancing girls. His next idea was to re-create a more bohemian club, like those in New York's artsy Greenwich Village. But after seeing the new movie, Gold Diggers in Paris, starring Rudy Vallee as a nightclub owner with a chorus line of American girls transported to Paris, he decided to do the same thing in reverse: He would bring Paris to Boston. What to name his vision? Of course. The perfect name was right there in one of the songs in the film. He would call his nightclub the "Latin Quarter."

Walters poured all his money—and that from friends and family as well—into the Latin Quarter. He got his liquor license the Boston way, by calling up an old friend, Police Commissioner Joe Tumulty, who in turn called up his friend Mayor James Michael Curley. Walters's club bespoke glamour and indulgence, resembling, as one former chorus girl put it, "a French boudoir" with draped walls and sophisticated décor. Weeks before the opening in October 1937, Walters was melting candles around the necks of empty wine bottles to give the club the feel of a French café. As he would later explain, "I throw the book at them. I try to give them the nightclub of their dreams." On opening night Walters walked in and, reaching into his pocket, gave the sixty-three cents inside to a busboy. "Now I can start from scratch," he said.

Walters's instincts proved correct. The faux French theme was an instant success, drawing people for the twice-nightly floor shows with girls in exotic, sometimes barely there dress. There were the bands (Renard was among those who played there) and entertainment, provided by stars like Jimmy Durante and Sophie Tucker and specialty acts. Faith Bacon, who billed herself as the original nude dancer, appeared there in 1939, clad only in a light dusting of powder and a diamond ring. High-kicking chorus girls opened the show with a song that Barbara Walters says she could still sing after a glass or two of wine: "We're stepping out to see the Latin Quarter: Put on your old beret. Let's sing the Marseil-laise and put your wine away like water."

Latin Quarter program. From the author's collection.

Menu for the Round Up. Courtesy of Kathy Alpert/Postmark Press.

Walters went on to open a Latin Quarter in Miami, and in 1942, one on Broadway in New York City. "It became one of the most amazing operations in Broadway history, and no one could figure out how Walters had done it," writes Robert Sylvester, in *No Cover Charge*. The New York Latin Quarter became "a national symbol of Broadway night life." The clubs brought the Walters both wealth and fame, and young Barbara loved going to rehearsals with her father, but she remembers the business was hard on family life. "Everything we owned, every meal we ate, the shirts on our back, so to speak, stemmed from the Latin Quarter."

Rose M. Arntz of Jamaica Plain remembers seeing the young Barbara and her sister at the club during chorus line rehearsal. At age ninety-six, Rose remains blessed with an ethereal beauty, with sapphire eyes bright in a porcelain face. A native of Connecticut, she started taking classical dancing lessons at age seven and by age sixteen she was performing in the chorus of a Broadway show. Under the stage name of Pat Palmer, she toured the vaudeville circuit as a straight lady for comedian Roscoe Ates. Her agent, Lou Walters, brought her and other chorus girls (in a troupe called the "Dancing Debutantes") to Boston in 1935 for a show on the S.S. *Royale*, kept anchored in the Fort Point Channel near South Station.

The boat was previously the private yacht of Sir Thomas Lipton, who had raced it in the America's Cup. The vessel was now owned by an outfit represented by Tommy Maren (who was the owner of the Cotton Club, where Charles Solomon was shot). Walters booked a show that included the Herbert Marsh and the Royale Marshals band, master of ceremonies Mickey Alpert, and his partner (and eventually his wife) Katharine Rand, and the Dancing Debutantes. Rose was paid $12 a week, not terrible wages for the time. Mr. Walters "was a nice person but when it came to money, he was a different person. He tried to get the cheapest and the best performers," she remembers. During her performances, she realized that the band's arranger and drummer, Royal (Arntz) Marsh, twin brother to Herb, couldn't take his eyes off her. When they got a chance to talk, she knew he was the man she would marry.

The Herbert Marsh band was one of many playing gigs up and down the East Coast from 1931 to 1940 and in venues like the Brown Derby, Casa Manana, the Round Up, and the Cocoanut Grove. Their booking at the S.S. *Royale* was exciting; there was a full meal service, dancing, and drinking, all with a spectacular view of Boston Harbor. The Marsh brothers, who had put their hearts into their band, were hoping for a long engagement.

But in September 19, 1935, a fast-moving fire broke out about 4:30 pm, forcing many of those on the boat to leap to safety in the water. The boat was destroyed and with it all the instruments and arrangements of the Herbert Marsh band, a devastating blow.

Still, the brothers picked themselves up, and Roy and Rose were married in New York in 1936. They returned to Boston where Rose danced at the Latin Quarter and the Fox & Hounds—often in alternating shifts on the same night. When she wasn't dancing, she was going to nightclubs with friends, places like the Cocoanut Grove and Mayfair. After Rose had a third child and Herb Marsh went into the Navy in 1941, the band was abandoned and Rose became a homemaker and costume maker.

Another dancer at the Latin Quarter remembers the club's opulent, rococo furnishings, the large dining room, and the stage where the "pony girls"—the twelve to thirteen chorus girls—danced, while the more exotic "show girls" struck poses. Eighty-year-old Laurie Cabot of Salem, Massachuetts, was a dancer at age seventeen at the Latin Quarter where, she claims, she was dubbed by *Variety* as "Boston's most undraped show girl." In the early 1950s, the Latin Club's floor shows were known for their theatrical costumes and three-times-a-night stage shows. Cabot remembers performing an elaborate homage to "The Red Shoes"; another night she wore a snakeskin-tight black body suit and danced solo to Ravel's "Bolero." Cabot saw Frank Sinatra, Sammy Davis, Jr., Buddy Hackett, and Tyrone Powers among the many stars who performed at the Latin Quarter.

Cabot only spent a few years dancing before her path took her elsewhere. People today "have no idea what places like the Latin Quarter were like," she says. "They have no concept of a dignified and elegant showplace where you can eat and drink. They think of Las Vegas shows where you walk in wearing sandals and bathing shorts. That's not the way it was in Boston. Everyone dressed up. There was no speakeasy feeling; the Latin Quarter was *the* place to go." Patrons dined and sipped champagne, fine whiskey, and cocktails. "I never saw a beer bottle in that place ever."

Surviving drink menus from the Latin Quarter reflect the era's drinking trends: martini, daiquiri, Bronx, Orange Blossom, Clover Club, Jack Rose, White Lady, and Pink Lady. A menu from the S.S. *Royale* also featured a Between the Sheets, Hop Toad, Lone Tree, Alexander, and Alexander's Sister. There was also an absinthe frappe and a mysterious Hornet's Hum. A menu from the Round Up featured a range of flips, from sherry to rum eggnog, as well as a Horse's Neck With a Kick. If a customer was undecided, a waiter might suggest a whiskey sour, Old Fashioned, Manhattan, or dry martini, as the club made more profit on these drinks, according to a sign posted for employees in New York's famed Stork Club.

By the 1930s and 1940s, Boston newspapers covered the events at nightclubs with the same avid focus that the media now gives to reality TV. *Boston Globe* columnist Joseph Dinneen wrote the regular features "Spilling the Beans" and "Inside Boston," and John A. Hamilton wrote

Rose Arntz, then known as Pat Palmer (second from left), rings in 1942.
Courtesy of Ronald Arntz.

"Time Out for Diners and Dancers." They filled their columns with promotional copy and gossip. One of the persistent rumors about Boston's nightclubs was that they were run by the Mob. That might be true of clubs in Las Vegas, Barbara Walters contends, but her father didn't deal with such folks. "I used to joke, sometimes, that I wish he had known them because we would have been a lot richer," she writes. The veteran newscaster might be just a trifle glib; certainly devious people like Charles "King" Solomon operated behind the scenes at various clubs. This was the Boston of Mayor Curley, after all, where the line between legal and illegal was vague. Edith Nussinow puts it in perspective:

> *Boston is a close family town and it has its own honor system and*
> *its own bad things. And if you're a Bostonian, you allow things to*
> *happen that shouldn't happen, you close your eyes to them. Like*
> *my mother said about the speakeasies and things like that: It was*

naughty but OK. It was illegal but OK. There was an excitement about these fellows who were the mobsters, almost a glamour (about them). There's no doubt my father had relations with these people. You had to have permission to do anything from some of these people. It was not an open town. There were hierarchies and rules and people in the know.

Whether Mob-run or not, nightclubs in the 1940s were a booming business in Boston, with 1942 looking to be one of the best years ever. A headline in the October 27, 1942, *Billboard* proclaimed: "Boston Niteries and Hotel Spots Expand Due to Best Biz in Years."

Within a month, that would all change.

Boston's nightclub era is overshadowed by one enormous tragic event. On November 28, 1942, a deadly fire swept through the Cocoanut Grove nightclub on a packed Saturday night killing nearly five hundred and leaving hundreds more injured and scarred for life. Restrictions in the aftermath of the Grove fire had a chilling effect on Boston nightlife for years. Across New England, clubs and restaurants were closed as authorities attempted to make up for inspections they should have been conducting before the fire. Musicians were out of work, and there was a drop in nightclub patronage from New York to the original Cocoanut Grove in Los Angeles. The beautiful draperies of the Latin Quarter were stripped away as nightclubs attempted to decrease potential fire hazards. Even when clubs began to reopen, there was a heightened sense of the danger of overcrowding—something that affects Boston firefighters to this day. As late as 1951, a Latin Quarter program insisted that the club's ceiling drapes were "absolutely" non-flammable.

Even without the chill of the Grove tragedy, Boston nightclubs would begin a slow decline in the late 1940s, as entertainment tastes began to change. The culprit had grown far more insidious than the cinema; now television kept people at home. Folks preferred their glamour in reruns. Boston's nightclub scene became a shifting carousel of names as clubs closed, reopened, and closed again. Lou Walters would eventually sell the Boston Latin Quarter to a group headed by Michael Redstone, a Boston theater operator who also owned the Mayfair. The Mayfair was shuttered, reopening as the College Inn Café in 1952, but it closed later that year in the wake of criticism by then-Archbishop Richard Cushing about the proliferation of "immoral floor shows." The Boston Latin Quarter closed in 1955. Walters also sold his share in the New York and Miami Latin Quarters to movie theater operator E.M. Loew; the New York club closed in 1969. Boston's Conga Belt was running out of steam.

The voice coming from the vinyl recording is unmistakable, although, as journalist and famed jazz writer Nat Hentoff writes in the liner notes, "The texture of her voice was as bruised and torn as her spirit sometimes became." Billie Holiday was in the twilight of her career, but she infused each of her songs with a range of moods, from the bitter anger of "Strange Fruit" to the mocking defiance of "Ain't Nobody's Business but My Own." Billie was bringing the blues to Boston in a remarkable performance at George Wein's Storyville, a jazz club in the Copley Square Hotel. You can sense the whispers of people in the crowd, the clink of glasses. What is even more remarkable is that at the time of the concert in 1951, Boston was a Mecca for the hep and the hip; indeed, New York and New Orleans had nothing on the cats of Boston. At places like Wally's Paradise, the Savoy, Morley's, the Hi-Hat, Estelle's, the Stable, the Jazz Workshop and more, the greats and near-greats would send rippling notes out into the night. Duke Ellington, Cootie Williams, Bennie Goodman, Dizzy Gillespie, Charlie Parker, Fats Waller, Stan Getz, or Count Basie would do a gig and then show up for a jam at an after-hours place. It wasn't just the music that made the scene so remarkable; it was that these clubs were some of the few places in Boston in the 1940s and 1950s where blacks and whites ate, drank, and smoked together.

As a kid from Quincy with a thing for jazz, Ron Della Chiesa would slip into Boston to catch the shows. "The thing that first hit you was the subdued light and the blue haze in the room," recalls the long-time Boston radio personality. "The music oozed out before you got in. There was a blue tinge to the air. Smoke and jazz go together. They really do. You knew you were going to be comfortable. Nobody was going to hassle you. There weren't going to be any fights. People were there because they had a mutual love of the music."

People would sip a beer, or a Seven and Seven, or a gin and tonic. "We drank crazy stuff like martinis, Manhattans, and screwdrivers," a former Storyville regular (now in her late eighties) tells me. "People don't drink like that now—you would have four or five mixed drinks." The smell of marijuana might drift in from the bathroom or the back alley. There was often food: ribs, fried chicken, grits, fish and chips, and chicken wings and waffles.

The 1950s were significant for Boston's black community, as an influx of blacks from the South joined long-time residents of African-American communities. Bostonians may have played a major role in the abolitionist movement, but black Bostonians had long faced deep-seated institutionalized discrimination here. Robert Woods, the lead author of the 1898 and 1903 South End Settlement House analyses of immigrant communities, saved his worst stereotypes for Negroes: "The Irishman may drink and quarrel, but he is first and last chivalrous...the Negro, loose as he is in character is usually gentle enough at heart." Blacks in other cities, such as Chicago, during the nineteenth century often became saloonkeepers, while in Boston, Perry Duis, the author of a major study of saloons in Chicago and Boston, concludes, "Blacks suffered discrimination that all but eliminated their participation in the Boston liquor business."

Which made the achievement of Joseph L. Walcott all the more significant. In 1947, he opened Wally's Paradise on Massachusetts Avenue. He had help from "Himself." The Barbados-born Walcott had worked as a taxi driver, and Mayor James Michael Curley, who was one of his fares, helped him get a liquor license. "In 1946, a black businessman simply did not have the clout or the capital to obtain the necessary permits and licenses to operate a nightclub," Richard Vacca writes in *The Boston Jazz Chronicles: Faces, Places, and Nightlife 1937-1962*, a remarkably comprehensive examination of this era. "Walcott had two reasons for opening a night club. First was to provide a place where black patrons were welcome." Clubs like the Hi-Hat admitted whites only—even if blacks were performing. Walcott's place was open to all, and the musicians of Boston flocked there. There were three bars, a full

The Hi-Hat in the South End. Courtesy the Bostonian Society.

kitchen, and a dance floor. Walcott later changed the name to Wally's Café, and he eventually moved to a smaller spot across the street, where it stands today—a treasure from the city's jazzy past.

By the mid-1950s, the civil rights movement was about to burst forth. Jailed for a burglary in Boston, Malcolm Little was learning about the Nation of Islam and transforming himself into Malcolm X. Martin Luther King, Jr., was doing his doctoral studies at Boston University, receiving his degree in 1955. At that time, the city had more than a dozen jazz clubs. A relative latecomer, Connolly's Stardust Room opened on Tremont Street in Roxbury in 1955 (on the site of the neighborhood bar known as Murray's Café), and remained in business for the next four decades. "Any jazz player raised in Boston cut his teeth at Connolly's," according to jazz historian Phil Wilson. "With Connolly's you never knew who would join you on stage."

When these bars made last call, the drinking was just getting started at the Pioneer Club, on Westfield Street on the South End/Roxbury line. Situated in a century-old building that had been a former rooming house and speakeasy, the Pioneer Club was one of the hippest, if somewhat obscure, spots in Boston in the 1950s. Owned by Richard Earle, then by Silas "Shag" Taylor and then Lincoln Pope, the after-hours bar was never exactly a secret, but you had to know someone to get in. Patrons had to ring a bell and wait for the doorman to open the peephole. If you were recognized, you'd be let into a small foyer. The door was closed and a second door was unlocked to let you in. Recalls Sarah-Ann Shaw, the first African-American TV journalist hired by WBZ in 1969: "Many Boston bars closed at midnight, and the musicians used to go to the Pioneer Club after they finished their gig and hang out, eat and drink, and sometimes play. There were booths and a bar and good food, and it stayed open until daylight." Athletes, reporters, even cops and politicians stopped in. Boston gangsters like Joseph "The Animal" Barboza, would drop by. *Boston Globe* reporter Bill Buchanan loved the place, writing, "It always seemed so delightfully naughty to order that beer for $1.25 at 3 am." The house beer was Miller, but many patrons sipped spirits, whiskey, gin, and vodka into the wee hours.

Miles Davis, Ella Fitzgerald, Sarah Vaughn, and Dinah Washington came by. "Some nights are the stuff of legend," Vacca writes, "for instance, when Duke Ellington and Louis Armstrong played duets until six in the morning or when Billie Holiday sang 'Detour Ahead' to a packed and silent room, tears streaming down her face." The majority of the patrons were black, but the Pioneer Club was one of the most integrated nightspots in the city.

The Pioneer Club closed in 1974, after heightened police scrutinty ensured it closed at the ungodly early time of 2 am. The building was demolished at the behest of the Boston Redevelopment Authority as part of the "progress" of urban renewal. "So now there is not a brick, a board, a leg of chicken or an empty bottle of Miller's beer...to indicate there ever was a Pioneer Club," Buchanan wrote mournfully.

By the late 1960s, Boston's jazz scene was largely gone, as musical tastes veered toward rhythm 'n' blues and rock 'n' roll. Joseph Walcott died in 1998 at age 101. Remarkably, Wally's Café is now run by his children. There is live music every day, from booked acts and latter-day cats who go there to jam. Walcott's grandson serves drinks from the tiny bar.

A *Boston Globe* entertainment column on May 13, 1964, by Buchanan captures in just a few paragraphs the dizzying culture collision of the 1960s. During that one week in the Boston area, Theolonius Monk was at the Jazz Workshop, Joan Baez at the Newport Folk Festival (she drove there in a hearse and slept in the back of it), comedian Phil Foster was at Blinstrub's, and the Donnelly Theater was hosting a closed-circuit TV broadcast of an NAACP civil-rights fundraiser with Nat King Cole, Harry Belafonte, Tony Bennett, Mahalia Jackson, and Barbara McNair. Gorgeous starlet Tina Louise was appearing in the musical "Fade Out Fade In" at the Colonial Theatre, but she would leave that musical to take on the role that would forever mark her: Ginger of TV's "Gilligan's Island." By the mid-1960s, the nation's tastes were in flux: rock 'n' roll was commandeering the radio dial, hemlines were rising, faded jeans were becoming the national uniform, and Americans began to expand their choices of beer and to sample fine wines in greater numbers. By 1968, the traditional nightclub was all but gone from Boston, except for one jewel.

In early 2012, Salem resident Heidi Webb came across a photo of herself as a young girl, tucked into a distinctive red, white, and blue folder. The memories came flooding back. It was probably 1961 or 1962, and her beloved mother was taking her only daughter into South Boston for a treat. Her mother, a wonderful ballroom dancer, used to talk about the old days when she worked in the General Electric plant by day and spent nights dancing and dining at the Latin Quarter or Hi-Hat. How glamorous it all sounded! And now her mother was taking her to a real nightclub for the early show. Heidi put on a favorite party dress, pulled her Mary Janes over her white ankle socks, and off they went to Blinstrub's Village.

Just walking into the two-story, brick and wood building at D Street and Broadway in South Boston was a thrill. The place was cavernous—it could seat up to seventeen hundred. Heidi felt like an adult, sipping ginger ale with a cherry in it, and waiting for the show to begin. That first time might have been the Lennon Sisters.

Or Wayne Newton. Or Chubby Checkers, who encouraged people to get on stage and do the Twist. She can't quite remember the details, but she remembers how exciting it all was.

South Boston, a residential section of the city to its south and east, is known for many things—its Irish population, its busing protests, and mobster James "Whitey" Bulger, its most notorious criminal. What it is not known for is its glamorous nightlife. Certainly the densely populated neighborhood reaching from Fort Point Channel to Castle Island and Boston Harbor is filled with bars and restaurants—some famous hangouts with murky pasts. What new residents may not know and what long-time Southie residents will not forget is how the place known as Blinnie's brought Rat-Pack style dazzle to D Street.

Postcard of Blinstrub's in South Boston, from the author's collection.

Stanley Blinstrub was born on Staten Island, New York; his parents moved to the Brighton neighborhood of Boston when he was three. By the time he was twenty, he was an experienced carpenter, mason, and painter, but he longed to run his own business. In the 1920s, he and his family decided to take over a shuttered restaurant in South Boston on West Broadway, its main thoroughfare. In 1934, he had bought up adjoining property and made plans for a larger nightclub. In 1952, he decided to try to bring in big-name entertainment and booked his first star, Patti Page. She was followed by appearances by Nat King Cole, Peggy Lee, Tony Bennett, Johnny Mathis, Johnnie Ray, Jimmy Durante, Robert Goulet, the McGuire Sisters, Eddie Fisher, Eartha Kitt, and Sammy Davis, Jr.

The club's exterior was odd-looking with a brick, Bavarian castle-like facade; the commodious interior made it a good spot for charity events and testimonial dinners. Blinstrub's often hosted charity events for now-Cardinal Cushing—the same Catholic clergyman who once railed about immodest floor shows at the College Inn Café. Everyone went to Blinnie's, for food (there was a daytime cafeteria), drinks, and to see the nation's top mainstream entertainers. Its reputation for good service and great shows was unmatched in the region. But it met a fate strangely similar to that of the Cocoanut Grove.

On the morning of February 7, 1968, smoke was seen in the building's basement, and employees quickly called for firefighters, who arrived a few minutes later. Five alarms later, flames were engulfing the entire building and threatening the congested neighborhood. The fire wasn't brought under control until the late afternoon. Jimmy Durante had been scheduled to perform at the club that week and sent ahead his musical arrangements, costumes, and comedy material from the last fifty years. All of it was destroyed. About 5 pm, a heartsick Blinstrub directed the removal of three safes from the smoking ruins.

The property loss was tagged at $1.2 million. Fortunately, no one was hurt. Unfortunately, Blinstrub did not have a dime of insurance. While he had liability insurance, he had dropped fire insurance in the 1930s, citing the cost. He told reporters that since the place was always kept up to code, was staffed 24/7, and he had installed concrete walls and brick floors, he thought he was protected. He vowed to rebuild.

Friends sprung into action, including Cardinal Cushing, who personally directed the staging of a massive fundraiser at Boston Garden for his friend. Where else but in Boston would a Catholic cardinal raise money for a nightclub? Stars like Connie Francis, Wayne Newton, Arthur Godfrey, the Righteous Brothers, and others headlined an evening that brought in $100,000 and a huge outpouring of support for the man behind Blinnie's. But even with the $100,000, the cost of rebuilding and starting from scratch was too much for the seventy-two-year-old Stanley Blinstrub. Plans for a new nightclub never materialized and he continued to work in his family restaurant business at the Old Colony House on Morrissey Boulevard into his eighties. He died September 28, 1978, at age eighty-one.

The corner of D Street and Broadway is now occupied by a gas station and fast-food place. As Ernie Santosuosso wrote in the *Boston Globe*, "Emerging from the debris of (the) flames was a cold appraisal that in terms of big-name entertainment, Boston is fast becoming a ghost town."

An era was gone. To be clear, there were and still are plenty of options for great nightlife in Boston. The greater Hub does not lack for watering holes, pubs, fine restaurants, live music venues, or even dance clubs where dressing up is part of the fun. But these venues are, for the most part, aimed at young people and college students, certainly not for families and those with gray in their hair.

Still, before we get too sappy about a mythical bygone era, let's recall the constant, lung-damaging cigarette smoke and the lack of compunction about getting behind the wheel of a car after a night of excess. Recall the sexism of the Rat Pack, the comedians who skewered women or purveyed stereotypes about African-Americans or other ethnic groups. Blinnie's patrons may have loved Nat King Cole and Sammy Davis, Jr., but South Boston was on the verge of exploding in rage at forced school busing that, however misguided in enforcement, was intended to level Boston's uneven racial playing field. You don't have to be temperance leader Cora Frances Stoddard to welcome a greater moderation in drinking habits, particularly when driving is considered.

Perhaps that is why today's craft cocktail events and the ladies of LUPEC cull the best of the nightclub era, taking a gill of its glitz and a dash of its glamour and leaving the rest to history.

MOSCOW MULE

(From the Latin Quarter.)

1½ ounces vodka
½ teaspoon powdered sugar
Juice of ½ lime
Ginger beer

In a mixing glass half filled with crushed ice
combine vodka, sugar, and lime juice.
Stir well. Strain into a tall glass filled with ice.
Top with chilled ginger beer.
Ornament with mint sprig and lime slice.

✳

2 BLOCK
AROUN
THE CORNE

UNITED
STATES
HOTEL

THE ROESSLE
BREWERY
PREMIUM
LAGER.

DONNELLY

OATNUTS

ARE ARE OATNUTS
YOU YOU

THE NEW
BREAKFAST FOOD OATNUTS

The ROESSLE BREWERY PREMIUM L

J.H. WALSH.
HARNESSES
& REPAIRING.

ATLANTIC AVE

BEACH STREET

WINES & LIQUORS

P.J. HAGERTY & Co

NES PORTS OUTH ALE.

ROESSLE BREWERY

Courtesy of Historic New England.

BOSTON'S BREWING PAST

The smell of beer brewing no longer wafts from these grand industrial build-ings, nor from the ten or so others that used to produce it in the Stony Brook corridor of Jamaica Plain and Mission Hill. Only our lone Samuel Adams Brewery can lay claim to continuing the neighborhood tradition.

–Michael Reiskind, "Two Grand Breweries,"
Jamaica Plain Historical Society, 1995.

Michael Reiskind of Jamaica Plain loves a good beer as much as the next Bostonian, but that's not why we are standing in front of the headquarters of the Boston Beer Company—the makers of Sam Adams lager—in Jamaica Plain. He's pointing out the smokestack that once puffed day and night from one of Boston's most remarkable compa-nies. The Haffenreffer brewery produced beer from about 1870 to 1964; its fourteen buildings and smokestack still stand. The plant's smoke-stack has been truncated, however, and reads "FENREFFER BREWERS." It could be worse, Reiskind says, pointing to the lighter-colored bricks at the top of the stack. Out of safety concerns the old smokestack was chopped to "FFER BREWERS," but after complaints, the smokestack was built up to accommodate a bit more of the old name, he says.

That's just one of the details that Reiskind likes to point out when he gives tours of the old breweries of Mission Hill and Jamaica Plain. A native of Montreal who moved to Jamaica Plain in 1972, Reiskind fell hard for the industrial brick landscape of his adopted community. A co-founder of the Jamaica Plain Historical Society, he set out to learn about the history of the many brewery buildings, some crumbling, some repurposed, and some entirely gone. Now he sounds the drumbeat for preservation. He rapturously comments on the clever brick design on the old Haffenreffer stable—pleasing to the human if meaningless to equines. He shows me where patriarch Rudolph Haffenreffer lived, just blocks away where he could see and smell the operation from his dining room. Haffenreffer may have even heated his home by running a steam pipe from his factory to his house.

Like the words "banned" and "beans," the word "beer" goes with Boston in an alliterative two-step. Puritans loved their beer as much as they loved propriety; the early settlers of New England often made their own brews, modeled on the ales, stouts, and porters of England. In 1637, Robert Sedgewick of Charlestown was given license to brew beer for the Massachusetts Bay Colony; according to tavern historian Gavin R. Nathan, this was the first license issued to brew in America. "The licensing seems like a bit of a formality, seeing he had already set up a brewery and had been brewing for some time," Nathan added.

Brewers mixed barley malt, hops, and yeast to make their ale; the result was deemed healthier to drink than water. Small and regional brewers operated throughout the country; after the Civil War beer began to emerge as the nation's dominant alcoholic drink. Ironically enough, the burgeoning temperance movement encouraged this. The abstinence crowd saw beer as a less potent, and thus less harmful, alternative to spirits. Around the country, the per capita consumption of beer rose from 3.4 gallons in 1865 to 20 gallons in 1915, according to the United States Brewers Association. While German immigrants in the Midwest launched the companies that would grow to dominate the market, self-sustaining New Englanders provided for themselves.

The Boston Beer Company, run by Irish immigrants, was founded in 1828 at D and Second Street in South Boston. Lawrence J. Logan, who was born in Galway in 1842, worked his way up to the head of the company by the early 1900s. The company catered to the taste of the Irish immigrants who would soon dominate the city and become the source of Logan's fortune. Across the city, in the area around the clear water of the Stony Brook, once a major waterway that flowed through Roxbury, Jamaica Plain, Hyde Park, and Roslindale, German immigrants began to set up breweries. To make lagers they used a different process than that of British and Irish alemakers by using bottom-fermenting yeast, a process that requires cooler temperatures, and more care and maturation. Top-fermented beer, such as ales and stouts, use yeast that rises to the top of the brewing tank and generally ferments more rapidly and at higher temperatures.

By the early twentieth century, there were more than thirty breweries in the Boston area by Reiskind's calculations, about twenty-five of them within a mile of Roxbury Crossing, another three in South Boston, three in Charlestown, and others in East Boston. These companies produced hundreds of thousands of barrels of beer yearly. In August 1900, a consortium was formed: the Massachusetts Breweries Company. Comprised of ten breweries, the consortium included American Brewing Company, Alley Brewing Company, H. & J. Pfaff Brewing Co., and Revere Brewery. By 1918, Moody's Investment valued the Massachusetts Breweries Company at $7,303,628, which would be roughly $111,157,832 today.

"These are the beers quaffed in Michael 'Nuff Ced' McGreevy's tavern after the Red Sox won their first World Series in 1903 and at Fenway Park when they won their last—for a while—in 1918," writes Mike Miliard in a 2005 *Boston Phoenix* feature on "The Ale Trail." "They were drunk in Beacon Hill townhouses and in Southie tenements, by Boston Brahmins and the hard-working German and Irish immigrants who made them."

These were major, bustling operations, employing hundreds of brewers, carpenters, barrel makers, deliverymen, and salesmen. The beer was delivered locally—particularly before national giants like Budweiser, Miller, and Schlitz moved in to make partnerships with local bars—and thus was consumed throughout New England. By the author's calculations using U.S. census data, in 1900, Boston had more breweries per capita than New York, Chicago, St. Louis, and Milwaukee, with 5.3 per 100,000 population compared to New York at 2.6, Chicago at 2.2, Milwaukee at 3.2, and St. Louis at 4.8.

The family-run German breweries were concentrated along the Stony Brook corridor of Jamaica Plain and Mission Hill. The area was served by railroad starting in the 1830s, and the brook (today almost completely hidden by culverts) provided the water. Land there was also cheap. "The work was arduous and the hours long. But for many German immigrants, working in a brewery was a coveted privilege. Particularly within German-American enclaves, the local brewery was often the nucleus of the neighborhood," wrote Carl H. Miller in "The Rise of the Beer Barons," a 1999 article in *All About Beer Magazine*. Thus, breweries were woven into the fabric of life in Jamaica Plain and Mission Hill, with owners, workers, and consumers all in the same area. Names like Pfaff, Houghton, Roessle, Rueter, Croft, and others were as familiar to beer drinkers of the nineteenth and early twentieth century as Busch and Budweiser are today.

The Burkhardt Brewery was one of the first German breweries in the Stony Brook area, opening in 1850. Gottlieb Burkhardt, a stocky man with thick salt and pepper hair and beard and a countenance as stern as Bismarck, nonetheless adapted well to America. His brewery was soon producing one hundred thousand barrels of beer a year with four kinds of ale and four kinds of lager. In 1870, he bought the Brook Farm property, the site of the famed Transcendentalist experiment in communal living located nearby in West Roxbury. Burkhardt eventually deeded it to the "Association of Evangelical Lutheran Church for Works of Mercy," which ran an orphanage on the spot for many years. In 1912, in partnership with the Red Sox, the Burkhardt Brewing Company, by that time run by the founder's son, brewed Red Sox Beer and Pennant Ale. The Sox won the World Series that year. (Coincidence?)

Beer and baseball mixed easily in Boston. H. & J. Pfaff, founded about 1857 by Henry and Jacob Pfaff, produced a popular bock beer. Charles Pfaff, son of Jacob who joined the business in about 1890, was closely associated with the Boston Braves; in 1916, when he was president of the Massachusetts Breweries Company, he was a director of what is

Boston shop advertising Pfaff's Lager Beer. Courtesy of Historic New England.

now considered Boston's "other" baseball team. The team's schedule was even printed on its beer labels, according to Reiskind.

The Haffenreffer brand was started by Rudolph Haffenreffer, a German immigrant who had worked as brew master of the Burkhardt Brewery and had married Burkhardt's niece. Haffenreffer purchased the Peter's Brewery and began operation in 1870. The company would eventually build a fourteen-building complex, with a main brewery, storage building, paymasters' offices, stables, and bottling plant. In the 1920s, the company bought the rights to Pickwick Ale from its original makers in Lowell; and after Repeal, started producing it. The brand was so popular that its plant was often called "The Pick" by older residents, Reiskind says. Legends abound about Haffenreffer. Supposedly there was a spigot installed where free beer was dispensed day and night. Babe Ruth is said to be one of many who appeared, pail in hand, to get a fill. There are rumors the spigot was operating as late as 1960.

Reiskind, who often leads tours of the old breweries, asks his audience to imagine beer making in Boston in its heyday. Workers, delivery wagons, and customers would have kept a constant flow of traffic near Columbus Avenue, Heath Street, and Amory Street; there were also streets named Germania, Mozart, and Bismarck to reflect the German heritage. The air would have been laced with the pungent odors of hops, yeast, slowly cooking grains, as well as the coal and wood smoke billowing from the brewery smokestacks and the rank odor of spent grain, left as waste.

In 1872, the Rueter Company, which produced ale and porters at its Highland Springs brewery, was considered the largest ale producer in the United States. Its Sterling Ale, with a high alcohol content of as much as fifteen percent, was popular for its potency. The company also won a first prize for ale in the 1876 Centennial Exhibition in Philadelphia. Rueter also served as the president of the American Brewers Association, which held off the temperance forces as long as it could.

Prohibition brought this thriving business to a halt. Technically, Prohibition was aimed at the evil saloon and its scheming barkeep (recall the powerful Anti-Saloon League), but brewers were viewed as agents of the enemy. Temperance advocates bemoaned the lobbying impact of the beer industry with as much vigor as those who complain about Wall Street's influence on contemporary American politics. The brewers had been able to weather prior crackdowns in the Commonwealth, including cyclical bans on alcohol and beer in the 1850s and 1860s, but national Prohibition proved too onerous.

In 1920, the Burkhardt brewery switched to producing cereal, but it eventually closed in 1929. Others turned to soda bottling or producing canned malted barley for home brewers, which was legal. The Haffenreffer plant continued to brew "near beer," light and dark libations with a lower alcohol content, including something called Pickwick Pale. Some of their near beers proved to be popular at places like Jacob Wirth's, which bought it by the barrel. One customer recalled, "Although lacking in authority, the flavor was authentic. Many of us first acquired a taste for beer from Jake Wirth's Prohibition substitute."

Only five breweries in the Stony Brook area survived Prohibition; they included Croft and Haffenreffer. The Boston Beer Company in South Boston had switched to making near beer, and although Logan died in 1921, the company was able to weather the dry spell. The company eventually shut down in 1957.

The Haffenreffer plant carried on until 1964, with the business passing to succeeding generations of the family, who all retained their palate for brews. Hasty Shields of Hamilton, Massachusetts, recalled how her father, Theodore C. Haffenreffer (the grandson of the original owner) who died at age ninety-one, used to taste a beer: "When my father tasted any new beer, the first thing he would comment on was how it was hopped. He would taste it, he would swirl it around his mouth, and he would say, 'Well hopped' or 'it needs work.'" Another grandson, August Haffenreffer, earned a degree in biochemistry from Harvard in

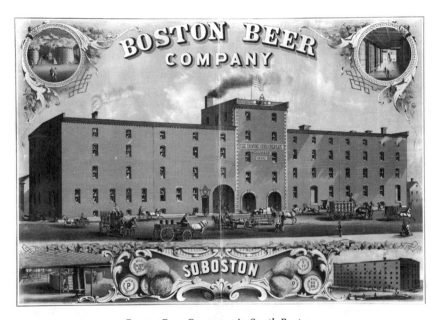

Boston Beer Company in South Boston.
Courtesy of the Trustees of the Boston Public Library.

1938 and helped concoct the Haffenreffer Private Stock Malt Liquor, nicknamed "Green Death" and "Haffenwrecker" for its potency and sale in forty-ounce green bottles. August Haffenreffer died at age ninety-four in 2010. Rudolph Frederick Haffenreffer—yet another member of the family—left Boston for Rhode Island where he established the Narragansett Bay brewery. This company bought out the Haffenreffer brand in 1964. After more than a century, the sprawling Haffenreffer plant fell silent, and the famous spigot went dry.

American Brewing Company in Jamaica Plain. Courtesy of Haffenreffer & Co.

Today, the glory of the years of Boston's beer barons can be glimpsed in the architectural flourishes of the remaining brewery buildings, many of which have been repurposed into condos, lofts, restaurants, offices, and shops. Reiskind will point out stained glass windows, ornate brickwork, and other details, but he personally mourns the loss of many other buildings, razed over the years. Haffenreffer and his fellow brewers didn't just build factories; they built structures that were monuments to their industry and their times. Many of them positioned their grand homes so they could look down into the Stony Brook Valley, over their breweries. The Rueter family plot in Forest Hills Cemetery was deliberately chosen so that it overlooked the family's breweries.

The glory of Boston's beer baron era may have faded, but Boston is back in the beer business. Jerry Burke of Doyle's still remembers the day in 1985: "This fellow came in with a six pack of beer. He announced, 'My name is Jim Koch. We're starting a new beer. Would you be interested?'...He said it's being brewed at the old Haffenreffer building. My brother Billy was very knowledgeable about beer. Billy tasted it and loved it." Doyle's became the first bar in the country to serve Samuel Adams Boston Lager.

The origination of Sam Adams is part of Boston beer lore, meaning that it has become the equivalent of a story told in a bar. Koch, a native of Ohio, supposedly found his great-great-great grandfather's beer recipe and decided to brew it. Koch bought the abandoned Haffenreffer plant in the 1980s, founded the Boston Beer Company— resurrecting the name of the South Boston company that had folded in the 1950s—and started brewing the beer he would name for one of Boston's greatest patriots. "I wanted Sam Adams the beer to create a brewing revolution the way that Adams the patriot created a political revolution," Koch has said.

Samuel Adams wasn't a brewer, but his family ran a malting business; that is, they made malt from barley, which was then supplied to brewers. The bulk of Sam Adams is brewed outside of Boston, but the company conducts research and brews small batches of beer at its headquarters in the former Haffenreffer site, which is open for tours and features a beer museum.

The Boston area now boasts a host of craft beers and microbreweries. The Harpoon Brewery on the waterfront in South Boston claims to be the first company to commercially brew and bottle beer in Boston since Haffenreffer closed in 1964. In 1986, Rich Doyle, Dan Kenary, and George Ligeti founded Mass Bay Brewing Co., and hired their first employee, Russ Heisner, a graduate of the University of California brewing program. The company now produces a host of beers including their famed Harpoon IPA and UFO Hefeweizen. Brewpubs, such as Cambridge Brewing Company, have revived the tradition of producing local beers for a local audience, recapturing the spirit, if not the massive output, of Boston's brewing past. Even the Haffenreffer brand still lives as Haffenreffer Private Stock Malt Liquor, produced by a company run by descendants of the family. Small-scale liquor distilleries have opened, including Bully Boy in Roxbury and GrandTen Distilling in South Boston. Boston Beer Company now plans to make whiskey with Berkshire Mountain Distillers in Great Barrington, Massachusetts.

Asked the most important question—how did those nineteenth-century beers taste?—Reiskind just shakes his head. "People ask me that all the time, especially home brewers," he says. He has no clue. Although some grand buildings of the breweries remain, the flavors live only in the imagination.

Advertisement for Jacob Wirth's.
Courtesy of the Trustees of the Boston Public Library.

The Crawford House in notorious Scollay Square.
© Massachusetts Institute of Technology. Courtesy MIT Libraries,
Rotch Visual Collections; Photograph by Nishan Bichajian.

NEIGHBORHOOD BARS: BOSTON'S HOME AWAY FROM HOME

The art of drinking is not acquired with the purchase of Old Mr. Boston's Guide to Mixing Drinks. *It is learned in the company of those who combine moderate intake with scintillating conversation.*

—Ray Oldenburg, *The Great Good Place: Cafes, Coffee Shops, Bookstores, Bars, Hair Salons and Other Hangouts at the Heart of a Community*

My favorite dive bar was O'Malley's in Union Square in Allston. It was the closest thing to a second family I had. You know who is gonna be there every night. You know exactly what's gonna happen. You have your drink waiting for you on the bar. You know what's gonna be on the TV.

—James Lynch, guitarist for the Dropkick Murphys, interviewed by Luke O'Neil for *Boston's Best Dive Bars*

In 1993, just hired as a feature writer at the *Boston Herald*, I spent my first evening at J.J. Foley's, a South End barroom. It was a Thursday night, the traditional night for *Herald* events. Thursday was payday. Thursday was near the end of the week. Even the greenest reporter could limp through Friday with a pounding headache; learning to write with a hangover has always been a required reporter's skill. About eight o'clock I strolled the few blocks from Harrison Avenue to East Berkeley Street and stepped inside a dimly lit room redolent of smoke and spilled spirits, its walls plastered with framed photos and memorabilia that bespoke of Boston's sports and political history. A campaign poster for Mayor James Michael Curley dominated one wall; one for Mayor Ray Flynn dominated another. There were signs pointing the way to Kilgarvan and Mangerton (in Ireland, of course) and to Dover Street. I looked around, slid up to the long wooden bar that ran the length of the room, and ordered my first beer.

At that time, the South End was in transition from dicey to hip, and this stretch of East Berkeley Street, with its choc-a-bloc garages and dingy storefronts was a no man's land. A pawnshop operated across the street. Around the corner from Foley's was the Pine Street Inn, a homeless shelter. Just a few blocks away, however, was Tremont Street, the edge of a trendy, gay neighborhood with theaters, art galleries, restaurants, and boutiques. Foley's, however, was worlds away from that milieu. Here, pressmen, reporters, editors, ad salespeople, and fresh-faced interns would gather for after-work drinks (for pressmen who had worked all night this meant first thing in the morning), and frequently there was a raucous going-away party for a departing staff-er. If the person were going to the *Boston Globe*, a bow tie would be among the inevitable farewell gifts.

Not that long ago, *Herald* employees could cash their paychecks at the bar, a service needed for those who worked odd hours in the days before the ubiquitous ATM. It was here that the women of the *Herald*—who often gathered for what we called a GNO (Girls' Night Out)—would tell the tale of the cuckolded wife who slapped her husband's paramour in the newsroom, a bawdy, gossipy narrative that grew wild-er with each retelling. It was here that the managing editor regaled me with the story of the grizzled editor who collapsed, bleeding, in the *Herald* newsroom and later died. The dark stain remained there for years until the entire carpet was removed. A jukebox would crank out rock 'n' roll, and even if there were only chips to eat, the Guinness would sustain you.

It was not unusual to find Mayor Ray Flynn or other politicians there. It was a place for off-duty cops and EMTs and other city workers. Soon after his election, Governor Mitt Romney, a famously devout, teetotalling Mormon, came by to stand everyone to drinks here. (I made it a point to be there that night. He shook my hand and assured me he was the equivalent of a liberal Republican.) At Foley's, someone was always buying someone a beer; no one was permitted to have an empty glass in hand. I soon learned to leave my coat in my car, else I would have to hang it outside for a day to let the cigarette smoke fully disappear.

Of all the bars I have frequented in Boston, Foley's is the one that feels like home. It's not that I went there often; indeed, compared to many *Herald* staffers, I was a lightweight, an infrequent habitué, showing up mostly for going-away parties. But never, not even now, years after I have left the *Herald* and so many of my former ink-stained companions have gone elsewhere, have I stepped through that door without a little voice in my head saying, "Welcome back."

This is the essence of the Boston neighborhood bar, a feeling as old as McGreevy's Third Base tavern (the last stop before home) and as potent as the myth of that place where "everybody know your name." The fantasy that was "Cheers," the long-running television series based on the Bull & Finch Pub, depicted a Beacon Hill bar as a drinking spot both familiar and entirely exotic. Where you met friends, fellow workers, your future lovers, your exes, the people who know you best, and people you will never see again. Where strangers and the strangely familiar all gathered for a drink.

This is a chapter about those places.

Let's not mince words. These are the places where the town gets wasted. And yet inebriation is often a side effect, not a goal, of the neighborhood bar. Ray Oldenburg in his influential examination of American public gathering spots, *The Great Good Place*, contends that, "The most important aspect of the drinking ritual is that it takes place among friends. The average American, like his or her counterpart elsewhere, is more likely to drink with friends than with relatives, neighbors or strangers." This is not to minimize the fact of alcohol overindulgence, sometimes unhealthy, sometimes fatal. As long-time Eire Pub bartender Martin Nicholson told *Globe* reporter Kevin Cullen in a 2010 article summing up his career: "I wonder, sometimes, how many people I served ended up at Pine Street. You're not serving Holy Water."

Patrons aren't drinking Holy Water, but there is often something mystical about finding your own Great Good Place. Boston certainly has had many. Student hangouts, gay bars, cop bars, black bars, biker bars. Buckets of blood bars where strangers ventured in at their own risk and drug deals were the least of a host of illegal activity. There are the bars steeped in tradition: marathon runners once recuperated at the Eliot Lounge; politicians curry votes at the Eire Pub. Sports fans head to the bars on Causeway Street, or to Daisy Buchanan's in the Back Bay; Beacon Hill goes to The Seven's Ale House. Dorchester has had dozens of neighborhood hangouts, places like the Dot Tavern, a small watering hole that blends seamlessly into the landscape of Dorchester Avenue. In Southie, there's Woody's L Street Tavern (glimpsed in the Boston-based blockbuster "Good Will Hunting") or The Stadium (the former Kelly's Cork 'n Bull) on Old Colony Avenue and Gustin Street, where the Irish Gustin Gang ruled in the 1920s. Boston's bars have nurtured both tippling artists and musicians. Fledgling punk rockers once sucked down cheap beer and shots at the Rathskellar, known affectionately as "The

Rat," a dingy bar and music venue in Kenmore Square where groups like the Dropkick Murphys played. In another memorable event in July 1989, a then-unknown Kurt Cobain and Nirvana played in Boston for the first time at Green Street Station (the site of the former Irish bars Kilgariffs and the Bog) in Jamaica Plain; Cobain had broken his guitar the night before—"over my head" as he told the crowd—and Jason Everman did all the guitar work. There was the time that Nathan Lane dropped into the Eagle bar or the occasions when pitcher Bill "Spaceman" Lee would stroll into the Eliot in his Red Sox uniform. There have been country-western bars like the Hillbilly Ranch in Park Square, which for more than thirty years showed Eastern bluebloods how bluegrass was played. There have been quirky bars, like Betty's Rolls Royce near Faneuil Hall where the flamboyant, irrepressible Betty Berman Arnold wracked up parking tickets for her yellow Rolls parked in front. Boston has had, briefly, a Playboy Club. There have been after-hours bars like Luigi's in the Combat Zone or the Stork Club in Charlestown and many others without names. According to a story told by former Associated Press newsman Dick Sinnott, when the S.S. *Andrea Doria* went down in July 1956, the AP's overnight editor managed to summon a photographer and three reporters within minutes just by calling the Stork Club.

On the other end of the scale are the elegant hotels, with places like the Merry-Go-Round bar of the Copley Plaza Hotel with its re-creation of a carousel that mixed elegance with whimsy. (The bar was a popular theme for postcards. I found one postmarked in 1942: "Dear Mom and Dad, I'm on the Merry-Go-Round but not getting too dizzy.")

Then there are the dearly and not so dearly departed: the famous Littlest Bar in Downtown Crossing, the Quiet Man in South Boston, Tim's Tavern and the Waltham in the South End.

Postcard from the Merry-Go-Round at the Copley Plaza Hotel, courtesy of the Trustees of the Boston Public Library.

Many members of the city's African-American community hung out at Estelle's or the Patio in Roxbury, Louie's Lounge in South Boston or Biff's in Dorchester, or at Slades, a bar and restaurant that opened in the 1930s and which featured music and Southern cooking—it had a reputation for the best chicken in town. Once owned by Celtics legend Bill Russell during the 1960, Slades Bar and Grill remains open today. Sarah-Ann Shaw, a legendary TV reporter who worked for thirty-one years for WBZ, personally liked to have a drink at a private club for black professionals located on Massachusetts Avenue in the South End; the club was founded by a group of black businessmen and open to women. In those days, "there was no rush for invitations to blacks to join the Algonquin Club," she noted drily.

There have been bars that bring together people of all types and bars that have unfortunately revealed Boston's past as a maelstrom of racism and ethnic hate, such as the South Boston bar that allegedly "celebrated"

Black History Month with an offensive display of jungle animals. Bar owners have told me of the days when wine was called "Guinea Red" and a bartender might break the glass used by an African-American—that is, if the black person would be served at all. As late as November 2010, a group of black Harvard and Yale alumni were denied entrance to a downtown club, alledgedly out of safety concerns. And yet during the 1940s and 1950s, blacks and whites were served drinks side by side at places like the Pioneer Club, George Wein's Storyville, and Wally's Café.

There have been Irish pubs—authentic and otherwise—German bars and tourist traps. There are new bars that pretend to be old, deliberately downplaying outside signage like the speakeasies of the past; you have to know where Saloon is to find it in Davis Square or backbar in Union Square.

The granddaddy of them all is the Warren Tavern in Charlestown, located in a building erected in 1780, just after the British burned Charlestown to punish those pesky revolutionaries. With a Masonic Lodge located next door, the tavern was named for Dr. Joseph Warren, killed in the Battle of Bunker Hill, whose likeness appeared on a sign outside "in his Masonic insignia as Grandmaster," according to a history published in 1888. By legend, Paul Revere drank here and George Washington supposedly stopped by. The Union Oyster House, which opened in 1826 on Union Street near Faneuil Hall, is another place that appears in all the Boston guidebooks as the country's oldest, continuously operating restaurant. Every neighborhood has its stalwarts—like Amrheins in South Boston, which dates to 1890—that have weathered the decades. But for every survivor, there are a dozen casualties.

Trying to capture the history of Boston's great good places, its corner taverns, jock bars, singles bars, jazz clubs, and its down-and-dirty dives, is as impossible as recording all the legends about Fenway Park.

All the stories are the same and all the stories are different. Consider the variations on the line: "A man walked into a bar." "A sailor walked into a bar." "A lady walked into a bar." "A politician walked into a bar." "A punk rocker walked into a bar." The set up is the same, the punch line different. But we must start somewhere, and so our first stop is J.J. Foley's in the South End.

Proprietor Jerry Foley's shrewd, flinty eyes are set in an angular face, topped by thinning black hair. Behind the bar, he wears a crisp white shirt, knotted tie, and apron, solidifying his appearance as a traditional barkeep. His movements are precise, efficient, and often his face is expressionless; he is a man who knows how to keep his own counsel. When he laughs, however, it's a sharp, welcome roar. Sitting down for an interview in the basement of his family's bar, Foley talks about his grandfather Jeremiah J. Foley, who came here from County Kerry, Ireland, around the 1890s and opened a bar in 1909. What he won't—or can't—articulate is why J.J. Foley's has lasted more than one hundred years when so many other Boston bars have faded away. "Hard work and prayers," is all he will say.

Like many Irish immigrants to Boston, Jeremiah Foley struggled to find work in the city. "People think Boston was very friendly to the Irish. It wasn't that way at all. They had to make their own ways," his grandson tells me. The bar, which was located on what was then Dover Street, catered to the huge number of Irish then living in the South End. Just down the street, near what is now Harrison Avenue, was the heavily Irish Kerry Village. Upstairs from the bar was Fay Hall, a social club for union members. It was here in September 1919 that police voted to go on strike in a momentous labor event that catapulted Massachusetts Governor Calvin Coolidge to fame for calling out the state guard

J.J. Foley's Kingston Street location in downtown Boston.

to break the strike. A plaque about this event now graces the bar's front entrance, and Jerry speaks of Coolidge resentfully, as if this were a grudge of last year.

That year, 1919, was also notable in Boston for another disaster in the city's North End. On January 15, a fifty-foot tall giant tank that held about 2.3 million gallons of molasses burst and sent a fifteen-foot tidal wave of the sticky stuff surging into the neighborhood. Twenty-one people were trapped and killed; forty more were injured. Urban legend holds that the tanks were overfilled to beat the requirements of the impending Prohibition. However, Stephen Puleo, author of the authoritative book on the subject, *Dark Tide: The Great Molasses Flood of 1919*, argues convincingly that the tank owners were using the molasses to make industrial alcohol for munitions, which would be exempt from the Prohibition and the Volstead Act. The tank owners tried to blame rabid anarchists rather than shoddy construction for the disaster. Decades after the clean up, North End residents insisted they could still smell molasses.

Over on the other end of town, bartender Jeremiah Foley was faced with his own personal disaster: how to support his wife and four kids during Prohibition. Asked how he managed, his grandson Foley fixes me with a look as revealing as a padlocked door: "He never missed a day's work in his life. He always went to work."

Always?

"Yes."

Did he have to pay someone off?

"He never bribed anyone."

Jerry vaguely conceded that there might have been a shoe store in the building and maybe it sold more than footwear. After Repeal, the "lights went back on." In 1959, the family opened another J. J. Foley's on Kingston Street in downtown Boston, and it is still run by the family. Jerry Foley's father eventually took over the business and then so did Jerry in the early 1990s, just as things were changing. Again.

Like so many areas in Boston, the South End has evolved over the decades, rich to poor, poor to hip. Once Boston's most fashionable address in the mid-1800s, the South End lost its cachet in the early twentieth century as the wealthy decamped for the newly created Back Bay. The area soon bustled with a host of immigrants and other ethnic groups, primarily Irish, Jewish, and black, who filled its tenements and lodging houses and worked in the area's light industries. And then things changed. Irish families moved up and out. I-93 was built, cutting off the South End from South Boston. By the 1960s, Foley's, as Jerry put it, became an oasis in a desert, or what others called a neighborhood bar without a neighborhood. Regulars would return and hang out, but that was not enough to keep a business going.

Foley's story could have ended there. The bar could have ended up like so many other places in Boston, even like entire neighborhoods, which have been lost to the forces of change. One of those areas merits special explanation. Let us go back a bit in time to a place called Scollay Square. In 1952, when the forces that would eventually raze the area were already in play, Pearl Schiff wrote in her novel *Scollay Square*:

> *What then is Scollay Square? Ask any sailor whose ship lays up in the Boston Navy Yard. Ask the girls who gravitate toward it night after night. Ask the rum-dum, the bookie, the horse player, the whore. Ask the Shore Patrol and the police officers of Station 3. Scollay Square is a mood, a rhythm. It builds up gradually through the day... to grand finale at midnight when the doors open wide, spitting their customers into the street.*

Scollay Square, named for the four-story Scollay Building, which was once one of the tallest in Boston, was centered at the crossroads of Tremont, Court, and Brattle Streets. A hub for the public transportation system, it served for decades as mercantile and wholesale business district, filling up with hotels, shops, and restaurants like the beloved Joe & Nemo's. Over the years, the businesses turned toward the risqué. The famed Old Howard Theatre, which opened in 1845, gradually shifted from Shakespeare and Mozart to burlesque. By the 1930s, Scollay Square was the go-to destination for sailors seeking food, flesh, or a good fight. A generation of Bostonians remembers cutting class to sneak into Scollay Square just to see what their parents were warning them about. As David Kruh writes in *Always Something Doing: Boston's Infamous Scollay Square*: "What these young men and women were skipping school to visit was a place completely unique in America. Located within its borders were tattoo parlors, burlesque houses, hot

The Lighthouse in Scollay Square.
© Massachusetts Institute of Technology. Courtesy MIT Libraries,
Rotch Visual Collections; Photograph by Nishan Bichajian.

dog stands, photography studios, nightclubs, restaurants, and one of the most famous theaters in the country."

David Kruh has the mellifluous voice of a former disc jockey. A New Yorker who came to Boston as a radio engineer, Kruh has had a multi-faceted career as a copywriter, radio producer, engineer, and webmaster. Currently a communications manager for a technology firm, Kruh has an insatiable passion for Boston's history. Through the stories he heard from relatives and old timers—including those from his uncle, a doctor, who patched up sailors who went to the square on shore leave and ended up bruised, battered, and ready for more—he fell in love with the lore of Scollay Square. As the keeper of oral histories that comprise *Always Something Doing*, Kruh has become the chief expert on that place and its time.

While his memory is based on research rather than personal experience, Kruh has encyclopedic knowledge about Scollay Square and the institutions that were part of it. The Half Dollar Bar, for example, had actual half dollars embedded in the clear plastic of the bar, designed to bedevil drunks who would try to grab the elusive coins. The Lighthouse was a piano bar, featuring a replica of a lighthouse over the entrance. It was popular among sailors and those hoping to meet one. One gay man describes the atmosphere: "People didn't have time to think about right or wrong. The war was going on. If you'd see somebody today you might never see them again…They didn't have time to think about whether they should do something." The Red Hat, a bar still in existence, had its crowd of regulars who told a story about a cat that would only drink beer. Kruh concedes that the stray cat likely subsisted on mice and only sipped the offered beer as an after-dinner digestif.

The Crawford House, located on Brattle Street, was a hotel, bar, restaurant, and nightclub. It served as an after-hours hangout for the so-called tuxedo crowd—the folks coming after the shows at the Latin Quarter and Mayfair, as well as for gay patrons. A circa 1940 menu showed a full complement of mixed drinks and cocktails ranging in price from sixty-five to eighty cents, including classics like the Manhattan, the Ward Eight, Sherry Flip, Singapore Sling, New Orleans Fizz, Stinger, and Zombie.

I ask Kruh to imagine what it was like to walk into the Crawford House in the 1940s. You would be first hit with a wave of warmth from the packed audience and a blanket of cigarette smoke, he explains. There would be the sound of laughter, clinking glasses, and conversation among both men and women. Despite the main attraction, this was a place where men could take their wives and couples would come on dates. There would be, however, large groups of sailors, perhaps ogling the cigarette girl selling overpriced cigars. Suddenly you would hear a drum roll and an announcer's voice would cause the audience to quiet. "Ladies and gentlemen, the world famous Crawford House is pleased to introduce the Queen of the Tassels: Miss Sally Keith." The band would strike up, and onto the stage would stroll a statuesque, platinum blonde in glittering beaded costume, with an eight-inch tassel dangling from each breast. Seemingly without effort the tassels began to spin, each in an opposite direction. And as the audience hollered and applauded, the performer would turn to reveal two more whirring tassels on her costumed buttocks.

This was Sally Keith, the real draw of the Crawford House, and a gal with a talent for twirling and self-promotion. Her act was naughty enough to draw in the crowds and nice enough to keep Boston's Watch and Ward Society at bay. She even had a special drink, the Tassel Tosser, named in her honor. The concoction of brandy, anisette, and triple sec cost a whole $1. But it was obviously a drink you could buy a lady.

Unlike what later emerged in what Bostonians called the Combat Zone—a warren of strip joints, peep shows, porn shops, and sleazy entertainment that appeared in the 1960s in an area near Boston's downtown and Chinatown neighborhood—Scollay Square was tawdry but not exactly X-rated. You would take a date to the Crawford House, Kruh asserts. You wouldn't take a date to the Combat Zone.

After World War II, as the sailors disappeared, the area slipped from bawdy to tawdry and kept on going down. In the 1960s, under the banner of urban renewal, Scollay Square's dilapidated buildings were torn down and replaced with the Government Center project, which included Boston's City Hall and the John F. Kennedy Federal Building. By 1962, the twenty-two streets that made up Scollay had vanished. Almost immediately Government Center's vast concrete plaza and fortress-like structures became one of the most despised places in Boston. The words "Scollay Square" became a symbol of an older, lustier Boston, a place of infamy now seen through the soft gauze of nostalgia. Sally Keith, then living alone in the Hotel Vendome, died in 1967.

Boston hit the skids economically in the post war years as well. This was the time of the beer and a shot, "a ball and a beer," as Jerry Foley called it. The most sophisticated mixed drink was a screwdriver. Certainly, there was fine dining and cocktail lounges; Locke-Ober, allegedly the place where the Ward Eight was first poured, carried on in undimmed elegance, but the city was changing again.

About this time, miles away in Jamaica Plain, another bar was about to change hands and become a Boston legend. Even if you've never set foot in Boston, you might have seen Doyle's Cafe, which has appeared as a backdrop in movies like "The Brink's Job," "Celtic Pride," and "Mystic River."

If Jerry Foley is close-mouthed, Eddie Burke, the retired Doyle's owner, is the opposite. A natural storyteller, he bubbles with anecdotes about the bar, the neighborhood, and the people and politicians of Boston. His brother, Jerry, is a bit quieter, but no less filled with stories and enthusiasm for Boston history. Since the 1980s, members of the Burke clan, including brothers Jerry, Eddie, Bill, and now Jerry's son, Jerry Jr., have run Doyle's on Washington Street in Jamaica Plain. Interviewing Jerry and Eddie on two separate occasions was like herding cats through numerous digressions and side stories, each more amusing—if not illuminating—than the last.

A man with a hearty figure and fine salt-and-pepper mustache, Eddie Burke talks about the family's early years helping his father run the concession business at Franklin Park. His own life goal soon became clear: "I wanted to be a saloonkeeper; that's what I wanted to be." He explains how Boston then had two kinds of drinking licenses: Taverns could stay open Monday through Saturday, 8 am to midnight, and women were not allowed to be served. Cafes had to serve food along with liquor, but could be open seven days a week from 10 am to 12:30 am and women could be served. Regulations are different today, but it is astonishing to consider that until the early 1970s, a woman could not legally be served a drink in a tavern in Boston.

By the late 1960s, Burke had bought the Stag Tavern in Jamaica Plain but was looking for another property. One day, he stopped off at Doyle's Cafe, a venerable watering hole established in 1882 by the Doyle family near Stony Brook in Jamaica Plain. Actually, the bar was virtually on top of the brook, which had been covered with a culvert. It was an excellent location for a bar, as it had been built near the many breweries that dotted the Stony Brook Valley from Mission Hill to Jamaica Plain. During Prohibition, the Doyles ran a grocery store out front and a speakeasy in the back. The Doyle and the Burke families were long acquainted; as Jerry Burke would later explain, a Burke patriarch had supplied liquor to the Doyles from his "candy" store during Prohibition.

As Eddie Burke tells it, "Billy Doyle says, 'What are you doing here?' (Because it's not my neighborhood.) I says, 'I'm trying to buy (a nearby tavern). 'You don't want that place, Eddie,' he says. He tapped the old bar. 'You want this place here.' 'I didn't know it was for sale.' 'It is.' I gave him a deposit on the spot for $5,000. And the rest is history."

Doyle's, run by brothers Eddie, Jerry, and Billy Burke, became one of Boston's landmark drinking institutions, surviving changes in the neighborhood, the economy, and Boston itself. That's because early on the Doyles decided to adopt a welcoming attitude toward all—including the folks considered "not from around here." They sponsored a lesbian softball team, the Dirty Sneakers. They hired a black cook, who once came out and challenged a customer who didn't like his cooking: "You complaining about my soup? You don't know a f***ing thing about soup." As *Globe* reporter and regular Alan Lupo wrote in 1994, "Doyle's bridges the old and new Boston," attracting regulars and newcomers, townies and tourists, Irish and ethnic, white and black. Jerry Burke expresses it a little more bluntly; suffice it to say, he'll serve anyone except for "assholes" who take offence by him serving anyone.

In the mid-1980s, the bar served the first glasses of a new brew, something called Sam Adams, produced by a fledgling Boston Beer Company. Over the years, the bar expanded to include the Michael Collins dining room, named for the Irish hero, the John F. "Honey Fitz" Fitzgerald Room, named for the Irish politician and the grandfather of President John F. Kennedy, and more recently the Tom Menino room, named for the Boston mayor.

Doyle's wall of fame includes a portrait of John "Honey Fitz" Fitzgerald, photograph by Shelby Larsson.

Jerry Burke gladly escorts the author on a tour of the bar. He shows off the photos of James Michael Curley, President Kennedy and Jackie, Teddy Kennedy, Senator Ed Brooke, and other Boston politicians. He tapped a copy of a newspaper article about the original John "Dropkick" Murphy, a former professional wrestler, who ran an alcoholic sanitarium at Bellow Farms in Acton starting in the 1940s. For decades, saying that you were "paying a visit to Dropkick Murphy" meant you were going to dry out for a while. Dropkick Murphy's shut down in the early 1970s, but the expression lingered and inspired the popular Irish punk band of the same name.

There is history everywhere you look in Doyle's: an entire wooden telephone booth; a portrait of Boston Strong Boy John L. Sullivan, who was a regular; large murals in which Ted Kennedy, John Collins, Maurice Tobin, John Hynes, and others are sharing a drink. A shiny brass rail, which can be glimpsed in a scene in "The Brink's Job" movie behind Peter Falk and Gena Rowlands, cuts through the main dining area, making a nice backdrop for tables. It was installed by a production crew in 1977 to set a scene for the film. Therein lies a tale:

"They did the whole joint up. It comes out beautiful," Eddie Burke tells me. "I ask, 'What can you leave here?' 'The brass rail.' They finish up. And the crew says, 'We're taking the brass rail.' 'You're not supposed to be taking the brass rail!' Cop says to me, 'It's theirs, they're taking it.' 'OK,' I says. I go off to the Stag Tavern. Three beers later and a couple of shots of cheap scotch, I got an idea. So we go around the back. The cops are across the street watching the joint. (We go) in the back door. They have this beautiful cappuccino machine (another film prop). We take it, run it down the trap door. Put it in a corner and pack beer cases all around it. And back out we go. Following day the phone rings. I can't get a hold of these guys for a week and the phone rings. 'Eddie, how are you?' 'Pretty good.' 'Have you seen the cappuccino machine?' I say, 'You know, there's a chance if you guys could find that brass rail, I could find that cappuccino machine.' They did. End of story." The brass rail remains.

Jerry's son, Jerry, Jr., and Christopher Spellman now run the bar and the older Burke is often there. He is still considered among the classic great barkeepers of Boston. Another is a man Burke remembers well, but who is almost forgotten today: Jimmy O'Keefe.

O'Keefe is associated with two legendary bars. Born in the Back Bay, O'Keefe found his calling as a bootlegger during Prohibition, working out of a drug store on Huntington Avenue. It was said, "Jimmy O'Keefe sold more booze there than he ever did aspirin." He helped elect Maurice Tobin as mayor but when Tobin, then a governor at the time, said he was too busy to help one of O'Keefe's friends, O'Keefe cold-cocked him. At least that's the story. In 1934, he opened The Dugout in Kenmore Square, a popular gathering place for sports fans and players. Red Sox manager Pinky Higgins drank there. So did Joe Cronin, Jimmy Foxx, and Jim Tabor. As a rookie, slugger Ted Williams drove O'Keefe's car. The police pulled him over one night. "Why are you driving Jimmy O'Keefe's car?" the officer demanded.

From the 1930s to the mid-1950s, O'Keefe also ran a nightclub and restaurant near the corner of Boylston Street and Massachusetts Avenue named Jimmy O'Keefe's Grill. Everybody went there—politicians, reporters, criminals. *Record American* reporter Ed Corsetti would pop in looking for stories and chat with the suave, handsome bookie named Adolph "Jazz" Maffie. Corsetti was shocked when Maffie was arrested along with nine others and convicted of the infamous million-dollar Brink's robbery of 1950 in the North End. The Brink's jury even paid a visit to the site of Jimmy O'Keefe's Grill, closed by then, to get a sense of how the crime of the century was pulled off.

O'Keefe continued to run the Dugout and befriend players, boxers, convicts, priests, cops, reporters, and cab drivers. "He knew everyone but the Unknown Soldier," a friend once said. O'Keefe died in 1987 at age eighty-three, asking that in lieu of flowers, donations be sent to the Pine Street Inn. The Dugout remains his living legacy, still popular among Boston University students.

If the Jimmy O'Keefe Grill was linked to the Brink's robbery, other bars have been linked to even more sensational crimes. On June 28, 1978, a janitor reported for work at the Blackfriars, a popular bar and disco located in Boston's Downtown Crossing. He made a gruesome discovery: five bodies, including that of the owner Vincent Solmonte and TV reporter John A. "Jack" Kelly, who was working there. The crime, which has never officially been solved, was likely the result of a drug deal gone wrong. In the 1980s, Triple O's bar on West Broadway in South Boston was a hangout for mobster James "Whitey" Bulger and his cohorts. Here, bouncer Kevin Weeks was befriended by Whitey and went on to be a player in his empire and later wrote a tell-all book about his time in Boston organized crime. In a notorious incident, bookie Louis Latif was escorted to Triple O's to meet with Bulger. His body exited wrapped in plastic. Another bar with a seedy past was the J.A. Café in Egleston Square, run by a fearsome bartender named Joe McGinnis, who died in jail after being convicted of laundering money from the Brink's robbery.

Doyle's had its brush with bad guys. In 1964, two men held up Doyle's while Billy Doyle was behind the bar. As the robbers attempted to flee, Doyle—a former Boston police officer—grabbed a pistol and started shooting, killing one of the men. As the Burkes put it, "Those were the only four shots Billy ever gave away." The "moon" that shines over Paul

Tending the bar at Doyle's, photograph by Shelby Larsson.

Revere's ride in a painting is actually a plaster plug from the bullet fired by the robbers as a warning shot.

In Boston, crime and politics can run in the same family: just consider the Bulger brothers. Likewise, the watering holes of Boston are the sites of bad behavior *and* incubators for Hub pols and voters. Recall the disapproving words of reformer James Woods in 1909: "Other things being equal, the man who has the greater number of saloonkeepers on his side will surely be elected." Woods would have been aghast at our current litmus test for presidential hopefuls—is he or she someone you'd want to have a beer with?—but there is something to this simple question. Plenty of bars in and around Boston have served as proving grounds for would be presidents. Not the least of which is a neighborhood bar in Dorchester, the Eire Pub.

With its gold letters proclaiming: "Eire Pub, Men's Bar"—a reflection of Boston's obsolete liquor laws—the Eire Pub remains a landmark in the Adams Village section of Dorchester. One of the first places to serve Guinness from Ireland, the Eire caters to the working men of the neighborhood, who pop in for a drink or a bite after work. On January 25, 1983, the Eire became ground zero in the battle to win the hearts and minds of the blue-collar, working class—a group that, by tradition, always voted the Democratic ticket.

It was a typical day at the Eire, with patrons unaware that Secret Service agents had been surveying the place. Then the door opened and President Ronald Reagan came in, entourage in tow. Next to him was Margaret Heckler, a former Massachusetts congresswoman whom Reagan would later appoint as ambassador to Ireland. As startled patrons looked on or were jostled by the press, Reagan was offered a pint of Ballantine ale. He took a couple of sips and put the glass back on the bar. Heckler reportedly grabbed the glass and drained it, which won her plaudits at the time but still seems somewhat bizarre. As photographers snapped pictures, the Gipper talked about his Irish heritage; his easy charm in the working-class bar solidified his "regular guy" credentials. The visit was brief but significant. For days afterwards, the media covered the pub like it had been the scene of an earth-shattering summit, pestering both patrons and manager John Stenson. One pub patron told a reporter, "They're not getting me on film. No way. I'm supposed to be somewhere else."

The visit created a political precedent. In 1992, Mayor Raymond Flynn attempted to re-create the same kind of publicity by bringing presidential candidate Bill Clinton to the Eire. Clinton merely *posed* with a Guinness; that he failed to drink did not go unnoticed by the regulars. In 2004, Senator John Kerry came to the Eire during his presidential bid as well.

The Eire wasn't the only whistlestop in Boston. Flynn led an almost unknown Arkansas politician to Doyle's, but Eddie Burke was too busy to meet this Bill Clinton guy. Jerry Foley, however, clearly remembers the time a young man who'd just delivered an inspiring speech at the 2004 Democratic Convention held in Boston dropped by Foley's. Four years later, Barack Obama was elected president. "I'm not sure what he drank; but he was a real gentleman," recalls Foley. "Haven't seen him since. He's been busy."

Today a brass plaque with Reagan's likeness gazes blandly from the walls of the Eire. Other candidates appear in photos, but only the Gipper has a plaque. Apparently both Kerry and Clinton have asked, "How do I get one of those?" They are told: Get elected president. And then return while president. Thus far, Reagan reigns alone.

While Reagan (and other candidates) will play up their Irish roots in Boston pubs, we should take note of the difference between an Irish-American pub and an Irish pub. Despite Boston's Irish immigrant past, many insist the 1980s was the era when true Irish pubs began to dominate Boston. That was when an influx of Irish immigrants began re-creating the pubs of home. One of the first to open was The Black Rose in 1976, and others followed. "Honest to God, the only bars opening in the 1980s and 1990s in Boston were Irish bars. I once counted thirty-nine," recalls Patrick Sullivan, who turned a Cambridge dive into the groundbreaking B-Side Lounge. Take your choice today among: Durty Nelly's, Hennessy's, Paddy O's, Mr. Dooley's, to name a few in the downtown area. Or head to Brighton to the Green Briar Pub, where Irish musicians regularly gather to play.

For another group of people in Boston at one time, bars were not only a place to feel at home, but also one of the few places where they could really be themselves.

Inside the Eagle bar on Tremont Street, unmarked except for the larger-than-life eagle spreading its fiberglass wings over the entrance, Roger Sampson, a bartender here for thirty-one years, greets the regulars by name. Sampson, genial and casual in T-shirt and jeans, fixes the drinks in plastic cups, even before customers order, and sets them on the well-worn surface of the long wooden bar. Overhead hang dozens of flags from countries all over the world, brought as offerings by patrons. A banner marking Queen Elizabeth's diamond jubilee sways prominently amid the profusion of colors. Photos, posters, and prints—many with naked or near naked men casting sultry glances from within the frames—and all manner of eagles dot the walls. With its tin ceilings darkened by age, mosaic tile floor, and perpetual dusk lighting, the Eagle radiates the aura of a neighborhood tavern. A tavern filled with gay history.

The Eagle—Boston Eagle is the legal title—is one of the oldest gay bars in Boston that still identifies itself as a gay bar. Before Rainbow coalitions, before AIDS was recognized as an epidemic, before "Will and Grace," before "Don't Ask, Don't Tell," the Eagle opened its doors to gay men for a pick-me-up, a pick-up, or a quiet drink among friends. "Eagle" is a code for a gay leather bar; there are Eagle bars from Amsterdam to San Francisco, unconnected except for the raptor signal for those in the know. The Boston Eagle was never a strict bruise-and-cruise fetish establishment. Sampson, however, still gets phone calls asking, "Is there a dress code?" "As long as you wear clothes, you can come in," he replies.

I am here to interview long-time Eagle owner Leo Motsis, a real estate investor who bought the property decades ago. He regards me with owlish bemusement, his eyes magnified by the lenses of his bold

Leo Motsis at the Eagle Bar, photograph by Stephanie Schorow.

Versace frames. He declines to give his age; the years, however, are etched in his face, and he answers my questions with weary good humor. In 1981, Motsis and a partner, Mario Mattei, bought a derelict joint once called the Record Café on Tremont Street. For the last nine months, the place had run as a gay bar with garish orange walls called House of Quagmire. Just before Motsis took over, the place was raided for staging orgies. Mattei, who had run the popular gay disco Chaps, took over as manager, got rid of the orange paint, left the original floor and footprint, and opened a corner tavern. There had been an Eagle bar in the Fenway, and Mattei and Motsis decided to use the name. The name didn't go above the door, incidentally. Mattei and Motsis merely installed a dramatic golden eagle. Unfortunately, a short time later, someone lassoed the eagle and yanked it from its perch. Motsis replaced it with a fiberglass figure purchased from the Brimfield antiques market; this bird was cemented to the wall.

These were the days when the South End was a poor, run-down area, plagued by crime and drugs. "Skid row," Motsis says. But the cheap housing attracted a thriving gay community who flocked to the local bars seeking drinks and companionship of long or short duration. The first gay bar in the South End was Elbow Room, Motsis tells me. Fritz, located in the first floor of a hotel, opened just after the Eagle opened; Club Café soon followed.

Gay Boston bar history goes back even further. In the decades after Prohibition, gay people (closeted or not) of all ages and classes mixed with straights in places like the Crawford House and the Lighthouse in Scollay Square and the Kit Kat Club, a former speakeasy, in Park Square or the Silver Dollar and Touraine Café on Washington Street or the Buddies Club on the Boston Common. An area between the Boston Common and Downtown Crossing on Lower Washington

Street was even dubbed Boston's "Gay Times Square." The Punch Bowl in Park Square, which was open 1947 to 1969, featured a dance floor, where women could dance with women and men with men. A flashing light would go off if police entered the premises, signaling patrons to switch to partners of the opposite sex or sit down. In the 1970s, Boston's lesbians went to Somewhere Else, a tough lesbian bar on Franklin Street, or to Saints on Broad Street—a straight bar during the day and lesbian bar at night.

One surivor is Jacques, a nightclub at the corner of Broadway and Piedmont (near the former site of the doomed Cocoanut Grove nightclub.) Jacques started to serve a largely gay clientele in the 1940s, according to *Improper Bostonians: Lesbian and Gay History from the Puritans to Playland*, a book published by the History Project, an initiative launched in 1980 to collect and preserve gay history and culture in New England. In 1965, Jacques's owner opened The Other Side, the first disco with same-sex dancing; it lasted until 1978.

The Playland Café on Essex Street, which opened in 1938, was perhaps the city's first bar opened specifically for gay patrons. Run by Agnes and Rocky Staffier, Playland had booze, music, and an anything-goes élan. Somewhat affectionately dubbed "The Upholstered Sewer," it became a hangout with a widely ranging gang of regulars including gays, transvestites, hookers, thieves, and other improper Bostonians. Eagle bartender Sampson remembers the "boosters" at Playland fondly; these were guys who came to the bar to sell everything from crystal bowls to copies of *The Joy of Cooking*. "I remember one day doing all my Christmas shopping sitting at the bar," he says, shaking his head at the audacity of the era's thieves. In 1998, Playland closed, falling victim to the forces of economics and urban renewal that closed many businesses in the district once called Boston's Combat Zone.

On the other end of the scale was the elegant Napoleon Club on Piedmont Street in Bay Village. Opening as a private club and speakeasy in 1929, the two-story establishment was purchased in 1952 by twin brothers Dick and Bob Amero, who started catering to an exclusively gay crowd. (When the *Boston Herald* reported this fact, the brothers quickly drove to their mother's hometown of Gloucester and bought up every paper so she would not see the news.) Like many men's clubs, the Napoleon had a strict dress code; it also had a piano bar, where bow-tied patrons gathered for impromptu concerts. Gray-haired men in three-piece suits and twenty-somethings in sports jackets drank martinis, vodka tonics, and wine—beer was only served on St. Patrick's Day. With its elegant décor and stained glass windows, its bold black-and-red décor, Napoleonic artifacts, and distinct logo, it was a favorite well into the 1980s. The Napoleon Club "wears its dignity like a diamond tiara," *Boston Globe* columnist John Robinson once declared.

By early 1990s, there were about sixteen gay bars in Boston. Sporters on Beacon Hill was usually packed, as was the disco Chaps on Huntington Avenue where, according to Sullivan, "dressing conservatively meant keeping your shirt on." These clubs and bars were not only places to go; they were places to come out. "They were the places where people met each other and felt safe—that's where you met your future lover—or lovers—and friends," recalled Libby Bouvier, a cofounder of the History Project. Gay bars and after-hours gay clubs were subjected to police raids and harassment, yet they were places of important self-discovery. "The first thing I ever did to identify myself as a gay man...was to walk into a gay bar," Robert David Sullivan wrote in 2007 in the *Boston Globe*.

Acceptance of gays by mainstream Boston came slowly. Four years before the definitive Stonewall riots in New York City that signaled the launch of the gay rights movement, city officials spoke of homosexuality as a social ill to be stamped out. In July 1965, Boston City Councilor Frederick "Freddy" Langone vowed to wipe out gay bars, saying, "We will be better off without these incubators of homosexuality and indecency and a Bohemian way of life." It was once unthinkable that regulars of Foley's and the Eagle—just blocks apart—would mix.

Motsis remembers how an opponent to a move in 1987 to relocate Chaps to East Berkeley Street railed about the possibility that "sissy" drinks like Brandy Alexanders would be served near J.J. Foley's. "Hey, Roger," he calls out to the bartender. "In thirty-one years, how many Brandy Alexanders have you made?" Roger thinks. "Maybe two or three." The 1980s also brought with it the scourge of AIDS, an epidemic that devastated Boston's gay community. In 1986, Mattei died of the disease, and Motsis carried on the business of the Eagle alone. Motsis recalls the first meeting of the AIDS Action Committee that was held in the Eagle in 1983, and he believes the first AIDS fundraiser was also held in the bar.

Over the years, many of Boston's gay bars have succumbed to the forces that close other kinds of Boston bars—changes in demographics, economics, and culture. The gay men who began the gentrification process of the South End found themselves priced out of the neighborhood. Instead of buying a drink for a good-looking stranger, people meet people through the Internet. The very success of the gay rights movement has, ironically, been a factor in the decrease of gay bars in Boston. As acceptance has grown, gay men and women don't need a separate space to socialize as much any more, Sullivan says. He compares the demise of the gay bar to the decline of other institutions, such as independent bookstores, record shops, and video outlets. Today there are perhaps six to eight bars in the Boston area that identify as gay.

The Eagle endures. About fifteen years after the golden eagle disappeared, Motsis got a call from someone who said, "We want to return the eagle if you won't prosecute us." "Just bring it back," he said. They did. The eagle has landed—now inside the bar.

Tracking just the past twenty years of Boston bar history is like throwing darts at a moving target. Old bars close but reopen with new names and new management. Some are repurposed—a Jamaica Plain bowling alley that dates to 1914 becomes the funky '50s retro hot spot, the Milky Way, in 1999, only to be forced to relocate a decade later without its candlestick pins to a refurbished building of the old Haffenreffer brewery. Neighborhood haunts are reborn as cocktail Meccas, such as Trina's Starlite Lounge and Green Street in Cambridge; Green Street proprietor Dylan Black has the oldest operating liquor license in Cambridge, dating to 1933. Other places live only in the hazy memory of patrons; the better the experience, the hazier the memory.

One of the challenges for Boston bar owners, say those in the business, is the high cost of operations here. The Massachusetts Legislature allows each community to issue slightly more than one full on-premise license per one thousand residents. This means that currently in Boston, there are 675 "all alcohol" licenses, which cover restaurants and bars, according to Jean Lorizio, counsel to the Boston Liquor Board. There are also 350 malt and wine licenses (also covering restaurants and bars). Those numbers have remained the same since 2006. No new full licenses are now being granted, but prospective owners can buy one from previous owners...if they can afford the cost of upward of $150,000. There are also complicated regulations for opening, closing, food service, and entertainment.

Boston's Puritan spirit of social control seems to rise from the dead periodically. Some bartenders remember the fearsome reign of Mary

Driscoll, who was on the Boston Licensing Board for thirty-two years and chair for twenty-two of them. Her stern countenance under a perpetually worn fancy hat was not a welcome sight when she was checking to see that bars were following the law. She was appointed to the license board in 1924 and retired in 1956 at age seventy-six. As guardian of the city's morals she was known for her impromptu visits to gay bars. Jerry Burke of Doyle's remembers her demanding that paintings of scantily clad women be covered up.

Despite Miss Mary Driscoll's best efforts, Boston has had its share of dives. The musician and drink master Brother Cleve remembers some of Boston's seedy bars of the 1980s with great relish; places like the Adams House on Washington Street and the Blue Sands—with its legendary blonde waitress Suzy, who at age seventy-five wore go-go boots and mini-skirts. She looked like Nancy Sinatra...from a distance. A survivor of that era is The Tam near the corner of Kneeland and Tremont streets, a watering hole featured on the cover of Luke O'Neil's *Boston's Best Dive Bars: Drinking and Diving in Beantown*. Luke O'Neil is among the chroniclers of Boston's new cocktail culture (along with *Drink Boston* blogger Lauren Clark), playing James Boswell to the Samuel Johnsons of the drinking crowd. When we meet, he explains the significance of the Moscow Mule in popularizing vodka in this country and signs a copy of his book with the decisive note: "Cocktails are history!" But this guy with the hip square glasses and fashionable face stubble also has a love for seedy corner joints where ordering a dry martini would blend as well as a three-piece suit. O'Neil relishes a good Boston dive bar, the derelict places where regulars walk in and stumble out, and the air smells of tainted breath and desperation.

Categorizing a place as the "best" dive is a kind of paradox, O'Neil acknowledges. To bartender and Dorchester native Jamie Walsh, a "dive would be a place you may or may not get out of alive. You're in a place, you mind your Ps and Qs, and you do your own drinking and don't bother about what's going on around you." And many bars in Boston once fit that description.

"Dive bars are like wounds on the body of the city, and patrons are like white blood cells flooding to the spot to fix it," O'Neil writes. "Big crowds of drinkers breathe a bar back into health, sometimes leading to the type of gentrified renovations that cover up any evidence that the wound existed in the first place. But cut off that blood supply and it hardens into a crooked scar."

If fire is the enemy of Boston's nightclubs (felling places like the Cocoanut Grove and Blinstrub's), condos may be the enemy of the well-loved but downscale neighborhood bar. The Quiet Man in South Boston was taken down to make way for a residential complex. And in March 2006, Boston lost a unique watering hole that had been in existence since the 1940s.

The Littlest Bar, located on Province Street in downtown Boston at the base of a parking garage, was hardly bigger than a parking space. Yet the tiny pub used to pack in the customers. "The door would open up, and you would think there was a four-alarm fire going on in the place because of all the cigarette smoke," Jamie Walsh recalls in an interview. Its official capacity was thirty-eight, but with a mere dozen seats it got close and chummy in a hurry. *Boston Herald* writer Dean Johnson notes, "Watching that many people leave at closing must be like watching clowns tumbling out of a VW Bug at the circus." Even its status as a Hub landmark, often mentioned in travel guides, could not save the Littlest Bar. In 2006, the property owners decided to use the space for a new upscale residential development and closed the bar.

The Littlest Bar. Renee DeKona/Courtesy of the Boston Herald.

But not for good. The owners of the Littlest Bar's liquor license opened a new (if larger) Littlest Bar on Broad Street that retains the flavor, if not the size, of the original. Over the years, other "lost" bars have been resurrected. A new version of McGreevy's Third Base Saloon, now billed as "America's First Sports Bar," was opened on Boylston Street in 2008 by Dropkick Murphys leader Ken Casey and film producer and Royal Rooters historian Peter Nash. Like its inspiration, it's filled with sports memorabilia and even has lights made from baseball bats. Moreover, it's only 1,200 steps to Fenway. The Green Dragon has been reborn on Marshall Street, stumbling distance from the latest incarnation of the Bell In Hand Tavern. Even Scollay Square lives, in the form of an upscale eatery on Beacon Street, which pays homage to the scruffy glory of that infamous place. No tassels, alas.

And, of course, J.J. Foley's endures.

What helped to save J.J. Foley's was the move by the *Boston Herald American* (later the *Herald*) to a plant on Harrison Avenue, just blocks from the bar. The newspaper's address was officially One Herald Square, but the staff eventually dubbed it Wingo Way after a promotional game instituted by the paper's then-publisher, Rupert Murdoch. *Herald* staffers soon found a home away from home at Foley's, and Foley's found a new band of regulars. "That was a great marriage we had with the *Herald*," Jerry Foley says. "We made a lot of good friends, from top to bottom."

I walked into the South End bar not long ago. The neighborhood had changed dramatically. I had left the *Herald* in 2005, and the *Herald* itself had moved in 2012 to new digs in Boston's Seaport District. Foley's, though, has continued to prosper in a rapidly gentrifying neighborhood. Upscale retail outlets have replaced derelict storefronts. New apartment complexes and trendy bistros cater to the young professionals moving in. Foley's has been remodeled, its space almost doubled with a new dining room, and there's now a full dinner menu. The pressed tin ceiling sparkles, the dark wood of the bar and tables gleams. I can breathe freely; the once unthinkable has happened. There is no smoking in Foley's. Years ago, Jerry saw the writing on the wall as the *Herald's* going-away parties multiplied. He retooled for a new generation, adding a restaurant while retaining the spirit of a neighborhood joint. From his place of honor, Mayor Curley is still smiling.

"The day of the tavern and the bar is over. You have to have a restaurant; you have to serve food," he tells me. "It's a different business than it was in the '50s, '60s, '70s, and '80s. People are more cautious. They're drinking less, but they're drinking better. They are drinking smarter."

And perhaps more tolerant. Patrons and employees of the Eagle often stroll down the street to have a meal at Foley's, and Foley customers occasionally head to the Eagle for a drink.

Jerry's sons are now joining him in a business that, at its core, hasn't changed. Jerry is supporting a push to change the name of East Berkeley Street back to the original Dover Street to better to distinguish the neighborhood. I sip a Guinness and talk with former *Herald* staffers who have wandered in.

It feels like home.

A BALL & A BEER

Order a beer and a shot.

Take the shot.

Drink the beer.

※

Bartender in action at Drink, photograph by Susie Cushner.

REVOLUTION
IN A COCKTAIL GLASS

*Stopped at the Crillon. George made me a couple of Jack Roses. George's a
great man. Know the secret of his success? Never been daunted.*

—Ernest Hemingway, *The Sun Also Rises*

*America could be described as the country where people mix their drinks
in strange, tantalizing combination and then consume them ice-cold.
It is the land of the brave and the home of the martini.*

—William Grimes, *Straight Up or On the Rocks:
The Story of the American Cocktail*

*Why do we call them craft cocktails? Because (makers) use fresh
ingredients. They are obtaining balance and depth in the cocktail.
You taste the spirits and you taste layers upon layers of flavor.
There is an enormous amount of skill going into these cocktails.*

—Alexei Beratis, Spirits beverage consultant,
interview, October 2011

When Jackson Cannon was a boy, his father—who considered Ernest Hemingway a literary hero—would read out loud from Papa's iconic novels. Cannon remembers being mesmerized by Hemingway's spare, staccato language as his father read *The Sun Also Rises*. But he had a question—and it wasn't about why Jake Barnes and Lady Brett couldn't be together. "Dad," he asked. "What's a Jack Rose?" To Jackson's amazement, his father listed the ingredients of this famous cocktail: Applejack, lemon juice, and grenadine.

Decades and countless cocktails later, Jackson Cannon still enjoys a well-made Jack Rose. With his Buddy Holly-esque glasses, slick hair, and precise elocution, Cannon hardly resembles another Boston bartender—the rugged, square-faced Patrick Sullivan whose accent could derive from nowhere but Boston. Yet something has tied Cannon and Sullivan together for the last thirteen years, and it comes in a chilled glass.

Growing up in Jamaica Plain, Patrick Sullivan was at home in a bar; his father worked as a bartender at the popular Midway Café. These were the days when the order was almost always for a shot and beer, usually a Bud. The faces along the bar were those of working men having a drink with friends and co-workers. Back then, ordering a cocktail would have been as common as donning a New York Yankees cap and asking for cup of tomato-based clam chowder with a side of foie gras.

Later, Sullivan went into the restaurant business. While he was working the requisite crazy hours and mad rushes that come with food management, he began to see something else at work. Passion. Passion for food, for dishes that delighted the tongue as well as filled the belly. Food that went beyond the steak and hamburgers to cuisine that was great to look at as well as to taste. And when later he decided to open his own bar, he wanted to continue that passion, to keep up the sense of exploration and discovery. And he also wanted a special something— something that would distinguish his place from the plentiful Irish pubs, dives, fern bars, pick-up joints, and out-of-reach upscale eateries that dotted the area. So with the help of a few key players, in December 1998 Sullivan opened up a small bar and restaurant in an offbeat part of Cambridge—the B-side, as he would explain. The B-Side Lounge would become a frontier in Boston's burgeoning cocktail culture. Now among the dearly departed, the B-Side Lounge recalled a tradition of the Colonial period when those who gathered in taverns discussed ideas that inspired a revolution. In this case, however, the revolution was about an old habit: drinking.

The B-Side may be gone, but you can still see the fruits of this revolution. Go to Congress Street in the Fort Point Channel neighborhood of South Boston. After you cross the bridge from downtown Boston, look to your left. Look hard. Eventually you will find a flight of stairs and a simple sign with hands holding various glasses and the words "Welcome to Drink." Go inside (that is, if you're lucky, as there is often a wait to get in), and you will be escorted to a seat at a long bar that zigzags around bulky support columns in one large open room. There's an industrial feeling, with the spare furnishings, the beamed ceiling, and the rough bricks and foundation stones exposed on the far wall. The configuration allows bartenders to talk easily with customers and for customers to talk easily among themselves. The drink menu looks sparse; just ask your bartender for something. Something classic, like a Manhattan. Something rediscovered, like an Aviation. Or maybe something you've seen on cocktail blogs, like a Periodista. Perhaps the bartender will make a beverage that is both exotic and complicated—like a Ramos Gin Fizz, with its blend of gin and egg whites. All eyes will turn to the bartender as she thoroughly shakes the mixture with quick, hard gestures over her shoulder. And when she pours the concoction— a snow-white avalanche topped with a twist of lemon—those along the bar may applaud. You might catch Drink's bar manager John Gertsen. With his crisply tailored shirt and vest and hayseed hair style, he could pass for a nineteenth-century barkeep, except perhaps for the hoops that jut from each ear. He sums up the high concept of Drink in a few words, "It's a cocktail party."

This and about a dozen other places in Boston, Cambridge, and Somerville are at the heart of Boston's Cocktail Nation. They represent a trend in drinking that Boston helped create. Boston most certainly cannot claim sole credit for what is now called the craft cocktail movement, but some of its more ardent pioneers came from the Hub. Like so many spawns of zeitgeist, this movement arose from multiple sources: cuisine, music, curiosity, and technology. It is a drink of contrasting ingredients—equal parts neo-lounge lizard, computer geek, and ardent foodie, garnished with nostalgia.

The genesis of the word "cocktail," like other aspects of drinking history, is a matter of speculation. Various sources attribute the word to a New Orleans apothecary named Antoine Amedie Peychaud who made bitters—alcohol flavored with herbal essences for a bitter or bittersweet taste, used primarily as a health aid—beginning in 1793. He would occasionally serve his bitters with spirits in an eggcup, or *cocquetier* in French, pronounced "cock-tayay." The word cocktail seems to have first appeared in print in 1806, when the editor of the *Balance and Colum-*

bian Repository—published in Hudson, New York—wrote in answer to a reader's query that a "cocktail is a stimulating liquor, composed of spirits of any kind, sugar, water, and bitters. It is vulgarly called a bittered sling and is supposed to be an excellent electioneering potion as much as it renders the heart stout and bold, at the same time that it fuddles the head." In the nineteenth century, a request for a cocktail often brought what we would now call an Old Fashioned (i.e., whiskey, sugar, and bitters with maybe a lemon peel or cherry). The words "cocktail" and "mixed drink" are often used interchangeably, but there have been mixed drinks for centuries. Wine was often mixed with water and Colonial Bostonians smacked their lips over all kinds of punch. Eventually the word "cocktail" has become associated with a blend of spirits, juices, bitters, sugars, and syrup.

Many assume that the cocktail became popular during Prohibition when vile homebrews were tempered with juices to make them palatable. Certainly that did happen, probably quite a bit. But what are now considered classic cocktails—the Manhattan, Sidecar, Jack Rose, Mint Julep among them—were popular long before 1920. A famous drinking manual published in 1862 by bartender Jerry Thomas called *How to Mix Drinks: or The Bon-vivant's Companion* specified how to make a Sherry Cobbler, whiskey cocktail, gin toddy, Tom and Jerry, as well as various kind of juleps and punches. Many of today's mixologists (and that term itself has been around for decades as well) consider the period after the Civil War and before Prohibition a Golden Age of cocktails. In the nation's saloons, bartenders experimented with different spirit formulas, tried them out on customers, and those that passed the test were handed down by word of mouth or recorded in how-to manuals.

While Prohibition did not stop people from drinking, it did dampen the inventive spirit of drink mixers, who did not have access to the better imported spirits or liqueurs. After Repeal, saloonkeepers scrambled to recall and make old cocktail recipes and to train a new generation of bartenders. Restaurants, nightclubs, and bars of the 1930s, 1940s, and 1950s soon revived a tradition of mixed drinks with exotic ingredients and clever names. A reprint of cocktail recipes from Lou Walters's Latin Quarter reveals formulas for the Gibson, gimlet, Black Out, and Zombie. One of the most famous cocktail recipe books emerged as a way to hawk a Boston-based product but ended up becoming a classic. Old Mr. Boston was a distillery built in Roxbury in 1933, during the heady days after Prohibition was sent packing. Bourbon, gin, rum, and other liquor were soon flowing out of Boston and into newly opened stores around the country. Founders Irwin "Red" Benjamin and Hyman C. Berkowitz figured that Americans needed to learn to mix drinks again—preferably with Old Mr. Boston products—and in 1935, the distiller printed the *Old Mr. Boston DeLuxe Official Bartender's Guide*, featuring a genial, if ruddy-faced, mix master dressed like he just popped out of a Dickens novel. The distillery and brand changed hands various times and is no longer located in Boston. The brand limps along with a line of liqueurs and cordials, but the guide, reprinted and revised, remains a bible for cocktail mavens.

Vodka was conquering America even as the Cold War heated up, what with the popularity of the Moscow Mule—a cocktail with vodka and ginger beer. Meanwhile, the vodka martini—considered a heresy by many—did battle with the gin martini. In 1953, a fictional spy spelled out exactly how to mix one. James Bond in *Casino Royale* asks his bartender to use "three measures of Gordon's, one of vodka, half a measure of Kina Lillet. Shake it very well until it's ice-cold, then add a large thin slice of lemon peel." He explains, "I never have more than one drink before dinner. But I do like that one to be large and very strong and very cold and very well-made."

A backlash against the fancy cocktail was underway. Leading the charge was the popular writer Bernard DeVoto, who in 1948 published *The Hour: A Cocktail Manifesto*. With a style halfway between a sigh and a sneer, he lauded the singular joys of a cocktail at 6 pm. A cocktail was a martini, a concoction of gin and dry vermouth. Or a slug of whiskey, perhaps over ice. That's it. DeVoto managed to be both snobbish and sexist about it, writing: "There are only two cocktails. The bar manuals and the women's pages of the daily press, I know, print scores of messes to which they give that honorable and glorious name. They are not cocktails. They are slops. They are fit to be drunk only in the barbarian marches and mostly are drunk there by the barbarians." He singled out drinks like the Bronx, once a popular drink at McGreevy's tavern, the daiquiri, and even the Manhattan as "an offense against piety." "A cocktail does not contain fruit juice," DeVoto pompously declared.

By the later-1950s, the martini ruled. The neon outline of a martini glass, usually with an olive and toothpick, became the very symbol of drink, as cocktail historian William Grimes notes. Strong, cold, and clear, the martini was possibly a reflection of how America perceived itself, speculates Drink's John Gertsen, a Hanover, Massachusetts native who studied biology and chemistry before he turned to bartending. In the 1950s, drinking was not about creativity and exotic ingredients; Americans were thinking about being a strong country that had gone through war and now led the world, he says. Clear spirits reflected certain purpose, a kind of "better living through chemistry" approach.

Maybe it was because baby boomers tried a sip of their parents' dry martinis, made a face, and never went back. Or maybe because cocktails seemed associated with a generation that looked down on rock 'n' roll. The 1970s were not a good time for cocktails. Writes Ted Haigh, a set designer whose obsession with old cocktail guides turned into the book *Vintage Spirits and Forgotten Cocktails*, "They still carried the scent of conservatism and the stale pointlessness of an old-man bar." And when a younger generation was experimenting with the buzz of marijuana and mind-blowing psychedelics, cocktails were hopelessly square.

Cocktails started returning in the 1980s, that is, if you can call Sex on the Beach, Fuzzy Navels, the Woo Woo, and Long Island Iced Tea cocktails. There was the Seabreeze, with its tasteless vodka and grapefruit juice that gave the illusion of health. There were Jell-O shots that promised oblivion and little else. There were the gimmicky "tinis and ritas" on menus, as restaurants dressed martinis and margaritas in gaudy, mismatched outfits. Or as Haigh writes, "Let's mix a little vodka and some liqueur shaken and strained in a stemmed cocktail glass and call it a fill-in-the-blank martini."

Meanwhile other forces were at work. There was a burgeoning interest in California wines, and craft beers were gaining traction. New trends in food, emphasizing fresh ingredients and careful preparation, were changing cooking styles, even in staid, steak-and-potatoes Boston. In the 1980s Dale DeGroff, a legendary bartender at New York's Rainbow Room, was taking an innovative, gourmet approach to making classic cocktails; in 2003, he published the influential *The Craft of the Cocktail*. In 2004, the Museum of the American Cocktail in New Orleans was founded. English teacher David Wondrich began writing about cocktails for *Esquire* magazine. Even the growing popularity of the Cosmopolitan—vodka, triple sec, cranberry juice, and citrus—was a harbinger of change to come, as Boston drink authority Robert Toomey notes.

Robert Toomey? He is the man better known by the title he adopted as a DJ and a musician, a moniker inspired by a reggae music seller and an old-time preacher: Brother Cleve.

Mixing drinks at Clio, photograph by Stephanie Schorow.

Cleve—even his close friends call him that—speaks softly and exudes quiet passion. Passion for playing music. Passion for composing. Passion for noir films. Passion for professional wrestling. And passion for the art of the cocktail. When he puts on his porkpie hat and retro suit, he is *the* poster child for the craft cocktail movement. The boy from Medford has come a long way since his family would take him to a favorite restaurant in Lynnfield. His aunt would always drink a Ward Eight; his mother would have a daiquiri. His father, a Rob Roy. His grandmother would have a Manhattan, and when no one else was looking, she'd let her grandson have a sip. "That is why a Manhattan is still my favorite drink to this day," he recalls in a long interview in his pleasant Dorchester home, cluttered with the kitsch that could have come out of a 1950s home bar.

Every modern mixologist, it seems, has an epiphany. Cleve had his in 1985 in Cleveland, Ohio, when he was touring with the group the Del Fuegos, a popular New England pop-rock band formed in 1980. It was November, and the band was having an early dinner at a local diner when Cleve flipped over the menu and saw a list of about seventy-five cocktails on the back. He recognized the Manhattan, even the Grasshopper, and a Pink Squirrel. And then he looked up at the bass player and asked a fateful question: "What the hell is a Sidecar?" Later that day, he slipped into a nearby bookstore and bought a copy of *Mr. Boston's Official Bartenders Guide*. There was a Sidecar recipe and many others, alluring and untested.

It isn't just that Cleve (and others who followed) simply made "old" drinks. They made drinks in old *and* new ways. They used fresh juices, not pre-packaged mixes. They found and used old equipment, shakers, and strainers. It was less about alcohol and more about attitude. They looked for unusual spirits from around the world. They looked for rare bitters—and then started making their own. Instead of buying syrups, they squeezed and strained fruits. They took the time to mash or muddle mint, slice off zests of lemon and lime, and thoroughly shake drinks.

After the Sidecar epiphany, Cleve continued to research and experiment and ultimately share what he had learned. It fit well with Cleve's persona—even as a punk rocker hanging out at the Rathskeller he drank Manhattans while others drank Buds or Rolling Rock. His obsession found common cause in the man called "The Millionaire," the front man of Combustible Edison, a band that formed in the early 1990s in New England. Cleve toured with the group. Combustible Edison spearheaded a movement toward retro lounge music—sometimes dubbed "Space Age Bachelor Pad Music"—performing music from

"La Dolce Vita," Henri Mancini, Morticia's theme from "The Addams Family," lounge classics from Juan García Esquivel, and their own brand of "crime jazz." Retro '50s and '60s garb and cocktails became part of the scene for both band and audience. Cleve likes to quote The Millionaire, "'Getting into cocktails was the most punk rock thing I could do.' Because nobody did it."

The group's first album, issued in 1994, featured a cocktail with brandy, Campari bitters, and lemon juice on the album jacket. The Combustible Edison Cocktail would be included by Paul Harrington in his book *Cocktail: The Drinks Bible for the 21st Century*, which was based on his columns for *Wired* magazine, one of the first magazines to cover the new cocktail movement.

In the 1990s, the must-read magazine for geeks might have seemed an odd outlet for a cocktail column, but it reflected the growing online community devoted to cocktails, building interest byte by byte as recipes were shared and queries posted and answered. Internet culture influenced a lot of things, the craft cocktail movement among them as enthusiasts launched websites and blogs devoted to the art of blending spirits. Late into the night, bartenders like Patrick Sullivan surfed the Internet for cocktail information, learning techniques from aficionados around the world.

Through the 1990s, Cleve's reputation as a drink mixer and music master was growing. He developed music and cocktail-themed events at places like the Lizard Lounge where he met a twenty-something Harvard divinity student and bartender named Misty Kalkofen. He became friendly with cocktail historians—people like Ted Haigh and David Wondrich. And he remembers meeting a young bartender named Patrick Sullivan who wasn't sure how to make a Negroni. Later when Sullivan, now enthralled with craft cocktails, asked Cleve for help in creating drinks for the new place he would open in Cambridge, Cleve was happy to oblige.

Sullivan, who had left a promising sales job to work in hospitality, didn't want to open yet another Irish bar, which were proliferating at the time. "I knew I had to come with something other than Bud Lights and woo woos," he recalls. He had a chance to take over the old Winsor Tap bar in Cambridge, a dive bar that would make other dive bars nervous. Looking up through a hole in the dilapidated property, however, Sullivan saw a beautiful, ornate tin ceiling. The old owner said the old ceiling had been covered up decades ago and was probably in perfect shape. "I was standing in an authentic cocktail room," he recalls. "I knew I couldn't go to my mother and say, 'Well, I'm just going to open this bar.' It had to be something different. I'd been reading about cocktails, and I love history and I ended up getting steered in that direction."

So, he assembled what *Boston Globe* correspondent and drinking enthusiast Luke O'Neil called a "dream team" that set into motion trends that "will be shaping the way we drink for years to come." Brother Cleve, Joe McGuirk, Dylan Black, and soon Misty Kalkofen were recruited to mix drinks. They started with six classic cocktails, and the word spread. The B-Side attracted the tech crowd, the gay crowd, students—even the Winsor Tap regulars stuck around. Restaurant people like John Gertsen from No. 9 Park would pop in, as did Jackson Cannon, a musician who had turned to bar management and who knew Cleve via the Lizard Lounge. "Some of us worked at the bar. Some of us sat at the bar," as Cannon says. The list of cocktails increased.

Cannon had also become obsessed with cocktails, their history, and their possibilities, starting with his boyhood interest in the Jack Rose. Cleve, Kalkofen, Sullivan, Cannon, and Gertsen began to meet monthly in something they dubbed the "Jack Rose Society." Since so many old recipes for classics were different, they figured, why not try to make a number of them and decide which was best. The first meeting centered on the Jack Rose, hence the name. Other drinks followed, including the Ward Eight. The discussions were enlightening and raucous.

Boston—at its heart—is a small town where neighbors, writers, politicians, business leaders, (and mobsters) all know each other. Same goes for Boston's cocktail crafters who seemed to work more in a spirit of camaraderie than competition. In its ten year run, the B-Side influenced scores of bartenders. In 2005, Cannon put together an astonishingly ambitious cocktail program for Eastern Standard, a large bar and restaurant that opened in a space once occupied by the Rathskeller in Kenmore Square. Cannon gambled that he could serve complicated, well-made, and expensive drinks—like the classic Whiskey Smash—to the area's young crowd as well as the demanding fans attending games at nearby Fenway Park. The Whiskey Smash—with its muddled mint and precision mixing that tastes best when drunk immediately—was "just the kind of drink busy bars that are five deep say they can't do" he recalls. But Cannon succeeded in making the Whiskey Smash the signature libation of Eastern Standard. In 2012, Cannon opened a new bar, the Hawthorne, named for a bit of historical research—the Hawthorne strainer, commonly used in cocktail making, was apparently invented in Boston. Cannon had proved that craft cocktails could be served on a large scale. In 2008, renowned Boston chef and culinary entrepreneur Barbara Lynch took over a large space in the Fort Point Channel neighborhood and with John Gertsen of No. 9 Park and other partners designed what would become Drink. Other neo-cocktail lounges have followed.

In contrast to the twists and turns of the Ward Eight, the growth of Boston's craft cocktail movement is remarkably well documented. In

Jackson Cannon serving drinks at The Hawthorne,
photograph by Stephanie Schorow.

February 2012, for example, Luke O'Neil, the author of *Boston's Best Dive Bars*, worked out an elaborate chart explaining the genesis of Boston's "Cocktail Creationists" with a reverential "who begat who begat who begat whom" approach. Published in the *Boston Globe* with a much longer version on O'Neil's blog, *Put That Shit on the List*, O'Neil charts the impact of the B-Side, Eastern Standard, No. 9 Park, and Silvertone on "offspring," including bartenders at Drink, Chez Henri, Deep Ellum, Highland Kitchen, backbar, Temple Bar, Trina's Starlite Lounge, the Blue Room, and others. It's a massive amount of data; O'Neil admits in his blog intro, "Anyone who doesn't find that sort of thing interesting should promptly skip this post, because it's pretty nerdy and soooo long I can barely even process it." Future alcohol historians may, however, be grateful for his geeked-out obsession. As Cannon says, "It's not a tree; it's a thicket of people who influenced each other and tried to help each other out."

Another chronicler of the period was blogger Lauren Clark, who also had her own kind of epiphany. A contributor to the *Boston Herald*, she had been writing about the craft beer world when she learned there was something new in town. "I went to bartending school. I knew about martinis and Manhattans," she remembers. "Then I learned the Negroni [made with gin, sweet vermouth, and bitters]. It is sort of a gateway cocktail; it seemed like this really adult beverage that a lot of bartenders knew." (Cannon, for example, calls the Negroni a "knock-knock" drink—something that signifies the person was serious about cocktails.) Through interviews with the area's budding mixologists, she found the new cocktails were "not the milkshakes that people drink because they don't like the taste of booze. They are drinks that taste of booze. This whole vast universe opened before my eyes, and I went 'Wow.'"

One name appears regularly in any discussion about Boston's craft cocktail history, a name that engenders the kind of awe reserved for the best of the best: Misty Kalkofen. Her bio might be the story just "told in a bar" but for a strange thing: it's all true. She *was* given the name Misty by her parents. She *was* a Harvard divinity student, working her way through school as a server at the Lizard Lounge in Cambridge when a bartender failed to show up and she was recruited on the spot. She *was* first trained by Brother Cleve. And she, Cleve, and Jackson Cannon once all lived in the same house in Somerville —"our little cocktail nation in Somerville," as she puts it.

On a recent night at Brick & Mortar—a new bar opened by Patrick Sullivan in 2012 in Central Square—Kalkofen was making her magic happen. With the dexterity of a juggling ballerina, often punctuated by a throaty laugh that Phyllis Diller would be proud to claim, Kalkofen deftly put together what only can be described as the perfect Jack Rose. Her sprawling tattoos say hipster; her manner bespeaks hospitality. "Bartending is much more than what goes into a drink," she says.

From that first impromptu night at the Lizard Lounge, Kalkofen was hooked on the craft of the cocktail. From working at bars in Boston and briefly in Key West, Florida, she has developed a reputation as an innovator, expert mixer, and teacher.

"Any drink she's ever made—whether a classic or one of her own—is just fantastic," Cleve says. Others simply call her the best bartender in town but, like trying to explain the elusive style of a great chef, they can't put their finger on exactly why. Kalkofen is now exploring the cocktail possibilities of tequila and mescal and their ritualistic uses in Mexican culture. Through the Tequila Interchange Project, she pushes for sustainable, traditional, and quality practices in the tequila industry. She did finally get her masters of theology and her two great loves—drink and spirituality—have finally come together. In some senses, she belongs to a long tradition of religious figures who make mind-altering concoction, from Native American shamans to Catholic monks who cultivated grapes for wine. And she still works behind the bar. "You have several times a night to make someone's day a little better," she says.

Classics are only part of the new cocktail movement. Some bartenders are pushing the envelope on ingredients, such as Todd Maul at Clio in Boston's Back Bay, which features cocktails with essence of Cuban cigar and burnt cinnamon stick. Beverage consultant Alexei Beratis, a former mechanical engineer who became a bartender when his company closed down says some believe you shouldn't mess with a classic cocktail; there's a reason they have lasted this long. But as new liquors, bitters, and syrups appear, the urge to create the next new thing becomes irresistible.

Beratis, for example, works with liquor companies to devise innovative cocktails by testing their products with ingredients like orange wasabi, sweet cream, and nutmeg. To make a cocktail that would go well with a clam bake, for example, he concocted a Rose of Corn: muddled corn with rosemary, lime juice, agave nectar, and tequila shaken, strained, and served with a sprig of rosemary.

Cleve has created any number of concoctions; when asked for a couple he would engrave on his tombstone, he cites two: the Peru Negro (with Macchu Pisco, Gran Classico, Sweet Vermouth, Amaro Nonino, and Bittermens Xocolatl Mole Bitters) and Maharaja's Revenge, made with Old Monk rum (an Indian rum with an unusual smoky flavor that he discovered on a trip to India), apricot brandy, and lime juice. At Drink, you can sip the Fort Point—with its blend of rye whiskey, Punt e Mes, and Benedictine—which was invented there.

The new cocktail culture can send enthusiasts on odd quests; they pore over old recipe books or hunt for unusual ingredients. Boston-area multimedia producer Devin Hahn set out on a quest to discover the origin of the cocktail called the "Periodista," an obsessive hunt he chronicled on his blog, *Periodista Tales*. In 2007, Hahn first tasted the rum-based drink, named for the Spanish word for "journalist" at Chez Henri in Cambridge. It was love at first sip: "The best Periodistas play a tango on your palate…It's a drink to savor in loud, smoke-filled pool halls or sip under the shade of a seaside palm." But Hahn wanted to know where the recipe came from, and his search took him through the ranks of Boston's mixologists, to the Tales of the Cocktail convention in New Orleans, and into dusty recipe books. He found his answer—which we won't spoil here—and in the process provides insight into how a group of Boston bartenders changed Boston's drinking history:

> *These people were never the in-crowd. They weren't the cool kids, those whispered of in hushed tones as they walked the halls. They weren't the beautiful people who gathered together on schoolyards to flex their adolescent muscles and vilify the awkward and brainy. These people were the awkward and brainy. They were the history geeks, the science nerds. They were the kids sitting behind the portables at lunch running lines for the school play. They'd grown up, and under the tutelage of the ultimate outsider, Brother Cleve, they'd found a calling to rally around. The cocktail renaissance had provided it all: history, rule books, arcane wisdom—historical costumes. Only a mistake of happenstance and culture had turned the nerdy kids' new obsession into the latest A-list trend. Ultimately, this was a band of outsiders who had found a place to come inside after all those years.*

It would be misleading to assert that Boston led the charge into the cocktail glass. San Francisco has always had a cocktail culture, and there have long been pockets in Los Angeles, Cleve notes. Cocktail lounges and neo-speakeasies appeared early in New York City. "We have a lot going against us," Cannon says, including the high cost of a Boston liquor license and the small population base compared to cities like Chicago. But Boston has a surfeit of what only can be described as smart drinkers: college students, faculty, young professionals, and gourmet foodies. Today, Boston's bartenders are well-known in the national and international cocktail community, tied by interests and the Internet.

Still, at its core, the new cocktail bar relies on everything that has always made Boston bars a home away from home. "I could teach you how to make these drinks," says Jamie Walsh, the man behind the bar at Stoddard's in downtown Boston. "That's not bartending. Bartending is

Cocktails at Drink, photograph by Susie Cushner.

talking. Knowing where the best steak is in Boston. Knowing where the best seafood is in Boston. Being able to talk to customers. None of us are reinventing the wheel. The reason we're making a cocktail is because a hundred years ago it was good."

Even when the B-Side was at its hippest height, there was always beer on tap for the regulars. Sullivan remembers hearing a group of them laughing about how their tastes had changed: "We came in here drinking $2.50 Miller High Lifes, and now we're drinking $12 scotches. You bastard!" Sullivan adds, "Is (the craft cocktail) for everybody? No, it's not for everybody. It doesn't need to be for everybody."

Cannon is well aware of the long heritage of the Boston bartender. "You can look at going to a bar as a political act. You can look it as ancestral worship. There are a dozen different iconic human expressions that dining and drinking in a bar are all about. That's why we wanted to make better drinks, that's why we wanted to make them the old way, that's why we wanted to create things we never heard of. That's all because of our devotion to the guest. That really drove the scene, not anything else."

One aspect of the new craft cocktail movement as practiced in Boston bars epitomizes Cannon's comments. It is a clear liquid placed before every customer and refilled with watchful regularity. The gesture says, "hydrate," and it also says, "stay healthy." It bespeaks of the new spirit of moderation; slow down and enjoy that $14 drink; feel the buzz and avoid the afterburn.

That's a lot of meaning in one glass of water. Then again, as we've seen, a lot can fit into a cocktail glass served in Boston.

MAHARAJA'S REVENGE

(Created by Brother Cleve.)

2 ounces Old Monk rum

1 ounce apricot brandy

3/4 ounce fresh lime juice

Shake with ice and strain into a cocktail glass.

Note: Old Monk is an Indian rum with a unique, smoky flavor, so no substitutes.

WARD 8

Juice of 1 lemon
½ jigger Grenadine
1 jigger Fleischmann's
   Preferred

Shake well with cracked ice.
Strain into 8 oz. glass.
Decorate with slice of orange
and Maraschino cherry.

CONCLUSION:
THE MYSTERY OF
THE WARD EIGHT

By now you may be thirsty. Thirsty for a foaming glass of beer. Thinking about a beading cocktail glass. Jonesing for your favorite libation. Or just maybe you are still thirsty for one more bit of Hub drinking history.

As promised, we return to the Ward Eight, the cocktail that reveals in its cool depths a story uniquely Boston. Be forewarned. The Ward Eight is an enigma wrapped in mystery, shaken with ice and poured into chilled glass. Like many cocktails—like the origination of the word "cocktail," in fact—many details about this once ubiquitous drink remain shrouded in myth. Untangling the threads of fact and fiction is much like deciphering a whodunit. Or in this case, a whodrankit.

To start, let's recount the history, as detailed by the place where it supposedly all began. Locke-Ober is a venerable fine-dining establishment, founded in 1875 on Winter Place in downtown Boston. Locke-Ober has long had the reputation as the place to eat in Boston even if, up until the 1970s, women were not allowed in the main dining room. (In the last decade, alas, that glory has faded a bit as tastes and times have shifted and downtown Boston has struggled economically.) In brief, its history begins in the 1870s, when entrepreneur Louis Ober opened a fine French restaurant at 4 Winter Place. In 1892, Frank Locke, a retired sea captain, opened the Wine Room café next door at 1 and 2 Winter Place. The two restaurateurs became bitter rivals, but patrons apparently would drink at one place and eat at another. In May 1894, a couple of wholesale liquor dealers bought both businesses and hired French chef Emil Camus. The combined operation was called the Winter Place Tavern, and the separate keys were ceremoniously tossed. In 1898, the place was sold to John Merrow, owner of the Revere House in Bowdoin Square, and Camus decamped for California. Merrow went bankrupt in about a year, and in 1901, a newly formed Locke-Ober Corporation took over. Camus returned and reigned over the kitchen for the next forty years. The name was eventually changed to Locke-Ober, forever joining the two rivals.

The Ward Eight cocktail is linked to Merrow's brief tenure, and its creation is attributed to an apparently skillful bartender named Tom Hussion. According to various accounts, Merrow brought Hussion to the Winter Place Tavern from the Revere House in the West End's Bowdoin Square. Members of the Hendricks Club political organization, which was controlled by Ward 8 boss Martin M. Lomasney, were accustomed to Tom's attentions and followed him to the Ober bar. According to a history of Locke-Ober, prepared by Sherman L. Whipple, III (and distributed by the restaurant), here's how the Ward Eight cocktail was born:

In November of 1898, Lomasney was running for representative in the Massachusetts General Court from Ward Eight. On the night before the election, a group from the Hendricks Club gathered at Tom's end of the bar. A toast to Lomasney's success at the polls on the following day was proposed, and all agreed Tom should compound a new drink for the occasion. The result, grenadine in a whiskey sour, was acclaimed and christened Ward Eight. It should be added however, that Martin Lomasney's responsibility for this joyful invention was only indirect, for he was himself an ardent prohibitionist.

That is the official Ward Eight story, circulated for perhaps a hundred years, and now spread across the Internet like Dunkin' Donuts across New England. It has a tangy balance of ingredients—Boston's neighborhood politics and inside-baseball shenanigans. And there's that lovely ironic twist at the end, hanging on the rim like a twist of lemon. But as noted in the opening pages of this book, this tale just doesn't quite hold together. We will unmix this drink bit by bit. Starting with: Just how do you make a Ward Eight?

Mixologists like David Wondrich, an author and cocktail columnist for *Esquire*, regularly study nineteenth-century bartender manuals for clues to original cocktail recipes. Through this research, Wondrich found a recipe for a Ward Eight in the 1926 edition of *The Cocktail Book: A Sideboard Manual for Gentlemen*, an extremely popular drinking manual that went through number of editions starting about 1901. The Ward Eight may have appeared in an edition as early as 1913, but it was definitely ensconced by 1926. The recipe calls for a teaspoon of sugar, juice of half a lemon, one portion rye, one tablespoon grenadine, and ice, adding, "Ornament with fruit and serve" and instructing mixers to "use a goblet."

The drink was widely popular in the Boston area by the 1920s. Variations on the Ward Eight recipe are found in bartending manuals from the 1930s to 1950s. The ingredients and their proportions vary—sometimes rye, sometimes bourbon was used, and sometimes there's a call for orange juice and orange slice. Some versions add a splash of club soda. The 1936 edition of the *Old Mr. Boston* guide to mixing drinks has an illustration of a "Ward Eight" glass but no recipe.

In December 1934, just after Prohibition, *Esquire* magazine writer Frank Shay lists the Ward Eight as among the top ten cocktails of the year and clearly identifies the drink as coming from Boston. In his view, the Ward Eight was among the pantheon that included the dry martini, the Old Fashioned, the champagne cocktail, the daiquiri, Planter's Punch, and the vodka martini. Drinks like the Bronx, Orange Blossom, Pink Lady, Fluffy Ruffles, Pom Pom, and Cream Fizz were deemed among the ten worst of the year. Shay gives this recipe:

> *In the Ward Eight they take the juice of a quarter lemon or half a lime, add the juice of a quarter orange. These are placed in a bar glass half filled with broken ice and a spoonful of Grenadine and a pony of Rye or Bourbon. This is shaken briskly and strained into a cocktail glass. In less informed sections of Boston there exist men who call for a larger portion of whiskey and have the potions served in a Delmonico glass that is brimmed with seltzer. Such outlanders wish theirs decorated with cherry, sliced lemon and orange. To me that final effort brings to mind a Christmas Tree out of season.*

But the Ward Eight recipe was truly a moving target. In 1934, G. Selmer Fougner began writing an influential wine and spirits column for the *New York Sun* called "Along the Wine Trail." Fougner ventured far beyond the scope of the noble grape, printing instructions for making wine and beer and mixing drinks, often calling on his readers for help. In those dark days before Twitter, Facebook, or—*gasp!*—the Internet, newspaper writers often asked readers to write in with information or suggestions. In 1934, Fougner put out a call for the recipe for the Ward Eight cocktail. He received, so he reports, about four hundred responses. He picked one and printed its very lengthy instructions:

> *The basis of a 'Ward 8' was a whiskey sour, the idea being to eliminate certain objectionable features of that drink. The Ward 8 was a distinctly warm weather drink, and should be so considered. It was always served in a large heavy glass of the type once generally used for beer—that is, with a large round bowl.*
>
> *The recipe for the original Ward 8 is: "Juice of one lemon, one barspoon of powdered sugar, a large whiskey glass three quarters full of bourbon (dissolved the sugar in the juice and whiskey), place a rather large piece of ice in the glass, add three to four dashes of orange bitters, three dashes of crème de menthe, one-half jigger grenadine. Fill glass with either plain water or seltzer, add two half slices orange, piece of pineapple and one or two cherries.*
>
> *When fresh mint is available the crème de menthe is omitted and a slightly bruised sprig of mint added with the slices of orange. This is an improvement.*
>
> *The amount of sugar should be regulated to taste, and likewise, the grenadine. The important factors are good liquor and good care in mixing. Properly made, the drink is very pleasant, although highly potent.*

So in less than twenty years, the Ward Eight won national fame and a multitude of imitations. There's a bit of a problem, however—and that's the grenadine, a reddish syrup made from pomegranates or other fruits. The name come from the French word for pomegranate, *grenade*. Wondrich and other mixologists insist that grenadine became widely available to bartenders only in the 1910s. That would shift the creation of the drink later or change its initial ingredients. Still, there was something called the Ward Eight as early as 1914; from about 1914 to about 1916, ads for "Ward Eight" liquor (at $1 a bottle and $10 a case) were run in the *Boston Globe* by the Santa Clara Co., a bottling and liquor dealer, on Washington Street. The ad declares, "We have notified (through the Press) all dealers in liquors that we own and control the brand 'Ward 8' which we have protected by registration throughout the United States. Any infringement on the above brand will be prosecuted." Modern-day mixologists speculate that this might have been just an attempt to capitalize on a popular drink (martinis were also sold pre-mixed in those days). Another company, based in New Hampshire, bottled and sold a nonalcoholic "Ward Eight" mixer that seemed to be aimed at the Dartmouth College crowd.

So what was actually in the original Ward Eight?

In 2006, the Jack Rose Society—that loose collection of Boston mixologists who gathered monthly to recreate old cocktails—held a meeting to consider the merits of the various Ward Eight recipes. "The Great Ward Eight Debate" was even chronicled by Anthony Giglio, a writer from *Boston Magazine*. Meeting at John Gertsen's Somerville home, bartenders Brother Cleve, Jackson Cannon, Misty Kalkofen, and Scott Holliday lined up the glasses, metaphorically speaking, and discussed possible ingredients. Lemons were commonly used, but would oranges, brought in by train from Florida, have been available? And grenadine was a sticky issue.

Jackson Cannon was, in particular, acutely aware of the issue of grenadine. When he first drank a Jack Rose, he found it not to be the glamorous imagined drink of his boyhood but a sickly sweet concoction as sophisticated as bubblegum. He blamed the commercial grenadine. Later, he made his own grenadine; he mixed and heated two parts pomegranate juice to one part cane sugar, reducing it slightly, and adding a whiff of orange-blossom water. That turned out to be a much better addition for cocktails.

Likewise, could Tom Hussion have created his own pomegranate syrup that would give the cocktail a special quality? Pomegranates *were* available in Boston in 1890s. A "market" article in a November 1898 *Boston Globe* showed oranges, lemons, and pomegranates—along with many other fruits uncommon today—were being sold. There's another possibility. Perhaps a bottle of a "new" syrup had come to Hussion's attention. Consider this: The 1912 edition of the *Federal Reporter* included the ruling in the case of *U.S. v. Thirty Cases Purporting to be Grenadine Syrup*, which was heard in District Court D in Massachusetts. Seems a beverage maker had shipped to Boston thirty cases of a syrup composed of sugar, citric and tartaric acids, and "certain fruits."

It was labeled "grenadine," but it was seized by the government on the claim that the name was misleading because it contained no actual pomegranate juice. The decision notes that "'Grenadine Syrup' has been an article of commerce in this country only during the last ten or fifteen years." This could mean that grenadine was used in Boston as early as 1897. So grenadine may have been a fairly new ingredient, hence that might be a reason for the nearly instant popularity of the Ward Eight. Incidentally, the court ruled that unlike the fairly common Orange and Lemon Syrups, a person buying Grenadine Syrup was not entitled to expect to actually get pomegranate juice, since the French-derived title was unfamiliar to most Americans. So much for truth in advertising.

That date of 1898 is curious for other reasons. That is because the creation of the drink is linked with Martin M. Lomasney, one of Boston's canniest, most charismatic political operatives from the 1880s to the 1930s. Lomasney was a contemporary of (and both ally and enemy to) the infamous James Michael Curley and John F. "Honey Fitz" Fitzgerald, the maternal grandfather of President John Fitzgerald Kennedy. Lomasney has fallen into relative obscurity; but that was his mode of operation. He largely worked behind the scenes. He is best known for his saying: "Never write if you can speak; never speak if you can nod; never nod if you can wink," or other more succinct versions of that sentiment.

Lomasney was born to Irish immigrant parents in Boston's West End on December 3, 1859. He never received a formal education; he worked as a lamplighter for the city and became involved with local politics, organizing Boston's Irish (and later Jewish) immigrant community. He was elected as a Boston alderman in 1893, and he later served terms in the Massachusetts State Senate in 1896 and 1897 and in the House from 1899 to 1902, 1909 to 1910, and 1911 to 1917. He returned to the Boston City Council from 1901 to 1903.

He never married. He lived with an aunt or his brother Joseph (who was also politically minded); in those days, that was called being a "confirmed bachelor." A lifelong Democrat, he also professed to be independent and would not hesitate to support a Republican if it served his purposes.

In 1885, he formed one of the city's most influential political clubs, the Hendricks Club, named for Thomas A. Hendricks, a vice president under Grover Cleveland who had given a stirring speech supporting Irish independence. The club was headquartered on Green Street in the West End; Martin Lomasney ran his real estate business on another floor. There he had an infamous safe, where, it was claimed, he had dirt

The Granara Saloon, City Square, Charlestown, circa 1915.
From the author's collection.

on every politician in Boston, providing him both power and security. Lomasney helped constituents get jobs and assistance; he worked with newly arriving immigrants and would go to bat for an Irish family down on its luck. He hated being called the Ward 8 boss, and when a newspaper columnist dubbed him a "mahatma," he preferred that title, although he had to first look up what it meant. Curley and Lomasney feuded for nearly twenty years, with each accusing the other of dirty tricks. Lomasney was a fierce promoter of Irish independence, which included fiery speeches at Democratic National Conventions.

He even charmed famed muckraker Lincoln Steffens, much to the dismay of the forces of "good government" in Boston, forces later derided by Curley as "goo-goos." Steffens, however, was impressed by Lomasney's interest in helping the public, writing, "Believe it or not, [Lomasney] was one of the best men I met in Boston. He was honest; he had intellectual integrity. He saw things straight and talked straight about them."

In November 1898, Lomasney may have been a sure bet to win a seat in the Massachusetts House. But that date is odd because although Lomasney himself might have been a shoo-in, his forces would suffer a huge defeat that November, a defeat that many declared would be the end of his influence. That was because Lomasney wanted his protégé, Daniel Rourke, to have a State Senate seat in a district that included the West End, as well as the North End and East Boston. Another Democratic faction, led by Mayor Josiah Quincy III, backed William J. Donovan. Rourke ran as an independent and lost.

Yet a month earlier, Lomasney's forces did win another race in a brazen act of political showmanship that was talked about for years to come. It happened on October 21.

As stated, one faction of the Democratic Party favored Donovan; Lomasney favored Rourke. But Lomasney as district chairman of the party had the power to designate the place of the nominating committee. He chose the Maverick House in East Boston (a place owned by P.J. Kennedy, the future grandfather of President John F. Kennedy) and the time of 4:30 pm—the names were due to the State House on Beacon Hill by 5 pm. (Some sources say Kennedy, a Lomasney opponent had arranged to have the meeting in East Boston.) Donovan's forces quickly booked up every room in the hotel, but a "salesman" had booked another room. Because the opposition controlled the ferries to East Boston, Lomasney's forces drove from the West End disguised as a funeral procession; there were even delegates tucked into a hearse. The "salesman" turned out to be a Lomasney supporter, and his forces packed the room, forcing the opposition to wait outside. Lomasney called the meeting to order; Rourke was nominated and business was concluded in seven minutes. An envelope with a certification was dropped out the window to a messenger who hopped a ferry to Boston. The opposition quickly held its own meeting in another room, nominated Donovan, and dispatched its own messenger.

The ferry carrying Lomasney's man mysteriously stalled—but that messenger turned out to be a decoy. Another envelope had been dropped to a college football athlete who raced to a private boat, which sped across the harbor. A bicyclist met him in Boston and, with Lomasney's forces stationed at corners to hold traffic, he raced to the State House. The certification was stamped at 4:49 pm. Donovan's messenger was hot in pursuit, also on a bike, but the chain broke and Donovan's papers were not stamped until 4:52 pm.

Rourke was declared the winner, but not for long. Eventually, the state ballot commission ruled for Donovan. More than twenty-five years later, Lomasney remembered the race with relish. "Yes, they licked us finally, but we made 'em fight, didn't we?" he told Thomas Carens of the *Boston Herald*. "Say, that was a great day. I don't remember how much it cost us, but it was worth every cent of it." And by the next year, Lomasney was putting together more winning tickets.

Could the celebratory drink been created in the wake of the great race? There's no evidence that pinpoints the creation of the drink to October. But the flush of the effort might have inspired members of the Hendricks Club to honor their leader the next month on the eve of Election Day.

Lomasney died in 1933, active nearly to the end, much mourned by his constituents.

One thing is certain: Lomasney was not a prohibitionist. He was definitely a teetotaler; he never drank a drop of liquor, and no drinking was allowed in the Hendricks Club headquarters. If someone was found to be drunk, he was escorted home. But Lomasney did not support the Eighteenth Amendment. (He also opposed women's suffrage.) Think back: promoters of enforced abstinence mostly hailed from the Yankee Brahmin class. Lomasney's natural allies were the workingmen of the district, the folks who spent their time at the corner saloon. He was not about to inflict his personal habits on his constituents. As a 1948 article in the *New England Quarterly* concludes: "He objected strenuously to Prohibition. He never touched the stuff himself and was heard to mutter frequently that liquor was the curse of 'our race.' But he knew the taverns in the West End *must* either close up or indulge in bootlegging and in either case he would be responsible for them."

Still, Lomansey was likely not there for the creation of the Ward Eight, and he may have had reservations about its name. The major biography of Lomasney, *Boston Mahatma* (1949) by Leslie G. Ainley, has no mention of the drink, nor is it mentioned in a multi-part *Boston Herald* series in which Lomasney dictated his memories to a writer. A 1951 article in *Holiday* magazine about Locke-Ober sheds some light; it's based on an interview with the management and staff of Locke-Ober with a great deal of imagination from the author George Frazier:

> *One night in 1898, a group of Hendricks members gathered at the bar and began discussing the next day's election, in which Lomasney was running for representative from Ward Eight. As the talk grew more and more animated, one of the men turned to (Tom) Hussion and observed that it would be a fitting and proper thing to invent a drink with which the boys could toast Lomas-*

ney's inevitable victory at the polls the next day. Hussion nodded and abstractly reached behind him for a shaker. Into it he put a jigger of rye, the juice of a lemon, ice, and a little sugar—the ingredients of a whiskey sour. Then, on a sudden inspiration, he added about an ounce of grenadine to the shaker. When he had given the mixture a vigorous whirl, he poured it into an eight-ounce goblet and garnished it with a half slice of orange. The man who had proposed the idea sipped the drink tentatively and then pounded his fist on the bar. "By God, it's a fine drink, Tom," he announced. "We'll call it a Ward Eight, me boy."

So far, that version follows the basic myth. But there's more:

Within a matter of weeks, the drink had become so popular that its potency began to assume legendary properties: in some quarters it was referred to as "the drink that'll make a girl forget her mother's advice." Apparently the only person who did not feel happy about the whole thing was Lomasney himself. According to one story, he is supposed to have had such misgivings about having his district immortalized in alcohol that he made several futile attempts to have the name of the drink changed to something less incriminating.

Alas, the trail of the Ward Eight goes cold there. There's comfort in David Wondrich's words to Devin Hahn, consumed by his own quest for the origins of the Periodista: "The moment of creation is shrouded in Stygian blackness, and if one should be granted a glimpse of it, one should be extremely suspicious."

So let's consider one more key question: How does it taste?

To answer that, let's go back to the Great Ward Eight debate by the Jack Rose Society. The group tried various versions, with and without oranges and varying the amount of the whiskey, both rye and bourbon, and grenadine. Nothing, however, seemed to suggest why the cocktail was so popular. "The really funny thing is that most of us didn't think the drink was very good," Gertsen recalls, somewhat ruefully. "Too sweet. We wound up at the end of the night saying, 'No more Ward Eights; let's have a Manhattan.'"

Indeed, back in 1934, *Esquire* writer Frank Shay came to the same conclusion:

> *Personally I do not care for this tipple but it deserves a place of honor because it has survived and because many otherwise reputable persons call for it. In case you happen to be in Boston ask for one but elsewhere you may not expect the perfected product.*

In other words, let's have a Manhattan!

And yet, says John Gertsen, "The drink is good. It can be made well. The trick like any drink is really good quality ingredients."

But alas, the classic Ward Eight may not be the most delightful cocktail to tease the tongues of modern drinkers. But, damn it, it's history. Do you eat Fenway Franks for the gourmet taste? Do you enjoy Revere Beach for its sophisticated beach attire? Do we say chowder or chow-dah, proper English be damned? Admit it: didn't you love that dirty water?

The story of the Ward Eight is more important than the actual drink. It is one of Boston's contributions to drinking history, a maddening, mysterious, strong and sometimes delicious bit of libation that somewhere, somehow, got its start in the neighborhood politics of Boston.

Dare we say it?

Cheers.

WARD EIGHT

(From Drink.)

3 ounces Old Overholt rye
1 ounce lemon juice
½ ounce simple syrup
4 dashes Angostura bitters
½ ounce grenadine
Top soda water

Place mint inside over-size vintage glass,
muddle, and remove. Shake rye, lemon, and
simple syrup in ice cocktail shaker. Strain into
prepared glass filled with crushed ice.

Measure grenadine, add bitters,
and "sink" into center of cocktail.

Top with soda water and garnish elaborately.

A GLOSSARY OF DRINKS, COCKTAILS, AND SELECT INGREDIENTS

COMPILED BY UNION PARK PRESS

As we have seen, drink recipes—like all recipes—evolve over time. What follows are broad strokes defining the cocktails mentioned in this book. Unless otherwise noted, the prevailing source is Old Mr. Boston DeLuxe Official Bartenders Guide, *1935. Neither the publisher nor the author makes any representation as to the quality of these cocktails, but merely include them as liquid artifacts. Cheers!*

ABSINTHE COCKTAIL

A cocktail made with absinthe, water, gum syrup, and bitters, then shaken with cracked ice and strained into a cocktail glass.

ALEXANDER

A cocktail popular in the early twentieth century, made with dry gin, crème de cacao, and sweet cream, served in a cocktail glass. There are many variations, including Alexander's Sister, made with crème de menthe, and the Brandy Alexander, made with brandy instead of gin.

AVIATION

This classic cocktail is made with lemon juice, dry gin, and maraschino liqueur, shaken with cracked ice and served in a cocktail glass.

BÉNÉDICTINE

An herbal liqueur produced in France, its recipe contains twenty-seven plants and spices. It is believed that Bénédictine is the oldest liqueur continuously made, having first been developed by Dom Bernardo Vincelli in 1510, at the Bénédictine Abbey of Fécamp in Normandy. Bénédictine is used as an ingredient in several cocktails, such as the Vieux Carré and the Singapore Sling. *Various sources.*

BITTERS

An aromatic flavoring agent made from infusing roots, bark, fruit peels, herbs, and other ingredients in high-proof alcohol. Historically, bitters were used medicinally, but soon became a vital ingredient in many cocktail recipes. For more information, refer to *Bitters: A Spirited History of a Classic Cure-All* by Brad Thomas Parsons.

BLENDED RYE HIGHBALL

Also called a rye whiskey highball, this drink features rye or bourbon, an ice cube, and club soda or ginger ale. It is served in a highball glass with a small bar spoon and lemon peel. If ginger beer is swapped in for the ginger ale, it becomes a Presbyterian. *Various sources.*

BLUE BLAZER.

From How to Mix Drinks, or The Bon-vivant's Companion, *by Jerry Thomas.*

BOCK

A strong lager (beer) of German origin.

BOUNCE

A cordial made with spirits and fruit, bounce was popular in the taverns of the American colonies. Typically made with cherries, bounce appears to have been a favorite of Martha Washington, who included the recipe in her journals. *Various sources.*

BRANDY EGG NOG

A drink typically associated with winter holidays and celebrations, Egg Nog has a long history. Made with eggs, sugar, brandy, milk, and topped with freshly grated nutmeg.

BRONX

Sister to the popular Manhattan cocktail, the Bronx is made with dry gin, French vermouth, Italian vermouth, and freshly squeezed orange juice. It's shaken with cracked ice, strained into a cocktail glass, and garnished with an orange slice. *Various sources.*

CHAMPAGNE COCKTAIL

Today the champagne cocktail comes in many styles, but traditionally it was made with sugar, bitters, an orange peel, and a lemon peel, served in a coupe topped with champagne and gently stirred.

CIDER

An alcoholic beverage made from fermented apples, cider was one of the most popular drinks of the Colonial period since it was considered safer to drink than water, which was often contaminated. Cider was particularly plentiful in New England, where apples were a major crop. *Various sources.*

CLOVER CLUB

An early twentieth century favorite, the Clover Club is a light pink drink containing lemon or lime juice, grenadine, the white of an egg, and dry gin. It is shaken with cracked ice and served in a chilled cocktail glass.

COBBLER

A drink first made popular in the nineteenth century, a cobbler includes a base spirit, sugar, and fresh fruit. As you can imagine, there are many different kinds of cobblers (see: Sherry Cobbler). "The cobbler does not require much skill in compounding but to make it acceptable to the eye as well as to the palate it is necessary to display some taste in ornamenting the glass after the beverage is made." —Jerry Thomas, *How to Mix Drinks* (1862)

COCKTAIL

The first known written definition for the word is quite fitting, so we'll share it here: "Cocktail is a stimulating liquor composed of spirits of any kind, sugar, water, and bitters—it is vulgarly called bittered sling and is supposed to be an excellent electioneering potion, in as much as it renders the heart stout and bold, at the same time that it fuddles the head." —*The Balance, and Columbian Repository* of Hudson, New York (1806)

Or, take Jerry Thomas's definition: "The 'Cocktail' is a modern invention, and is generally used on fishing and other sporting parties, although some *patients* insist that it is good in the morning as a tonic." —Jerry Thomas, *How to Mix Drinks* (1862)

COLUMBIA SKIN

Known in Boston as the Columbia Skin, but elsewhere called the Whiskey Skin, this whiskey-based cocktail includes a bit of sugar, boiling water, whiskey, and a garnish of a lemon peel. *Lupecboston.com*

COSMOPOLITAN

A relatively new cocktail, the Cosmopolitan (or "Cosmo") was invented sometime in the 1970s or 1980s, and was made exceedingly popular by the TV show *Sex and the City*. The drink includes vodka, Cointreau, cranberry juice, and lime juice and is served in a chilled cocktail glass, sometimes with a sugar-frosted rim. *Various sources*

CREAM FIZZ

A sweet and creamy libation made with lemon juice, powdered sugar, dry gin, and cream.

CRUSTA

We'll let famed bartender Jerry Thomas tell you about this one: "Crusta is made the same as a fancy cocktail with a little lemon juice and a small lump of ice added. First mix the ingredients in a small tumbler, then take a fancy red wine glass, rub a sliced lemon around the rim of the same and dip it in pulverized white sugar so that the sugar will adhere to the edge of the glass. Pare half a lemon the same as you would an apple all in one piece so that the paring will fit in the wine glass... and strain the crusta from the tumbler into it. Then smile."
—Jerry Thomas, *How to Mix Drinks* (1862)

FLIP

The flip has been around for centuries, and in this country it was a drink that was once made with beer, sugar, molasses, or dried pumpkin to taste and a few dashes of rum. A red-hot poker was then thrust into the mug, and stirred, resulting in a liquid that would foam and bubble and taste extraordinarily bitter. (For more: *Historic Taverns of Boston: 370 Years of Tavern History in One Definitive Guide* by Gavin R. Nathan.) The flip changed over time, however, with the elimination of beer and the addition of more sugar and eggs. "The essential in flips of all sorts is to produce the smoothness by repeated pouring back and forward between two vessels and beating up the eggs well in the first instance..." —Jerry Thomas, *How to Mix Drinks* (1862)

FLUFFY RUFFLES

A cocktail made with rum, Italian vermouth, and lime stirred with cracked ice and strained into cocktail glass. *Various sources.*

FUZZY NAVEL

A classic 1980s cocktail (if there is such a thing) containing peach schnapps, orange juice, and ice cubes. *Various sources.*

GIBSON

A relative to the dry martini, the Gibson is made with either vodka or gin, dry vermouth and is served in a chilled glass and garnished with a cocktail onion (instead of an olive). *Esquire.com*

GIMLET

A cocktail traced to the 1920s, the Gimlet is traditionally made with dry gin, lime juice, and Rose's lime cordial. *Various sources.*

GIN BUCK

A mid-twentieth century drink that has fallen out of the mainstream, the Gin Buck is made with lemon juice, dry gin, and ginger ale. Today, those who drink it use ginger beer, for a spicier kick truer to the original. *Various sources.*

GIN FIZZ

Part of a larger fizz family of cocktails, the Gin Fizz is made with lemon juice, sugar, and gin. It is then shaken with ice and strained into a glass and topped with club soda. *Various sources.*

GIN SLING

Historically, a sling was made with spirits, sugar, and water. *Mr. Boston* (1935) suggests that a Gin Sling be made with gin, sugar, water, apricot nectar liqueur, and a cube of ice, and served in a glass with soda water.

GIN SOUR

This drink is made with dry gin, lemon juice, and powdered sugar, shaken well with cracked ice and strained into a Delmonico glass. It is then filled with soda water and decorated with a half slice of lemon.

GRASSHOPPER

A sweet after-dinner drink, the Grasshopper includes green crème de menthe, white crème de cacao, and light cream. *Various sources.*

HIGHBALL

A family of drinks consisting of a base alcohol and a mixer such as soda water or ginger ale, served in a tall glass, such as a Scotch and soda, a gin and tonic, or a Moscow Mule. *Various sources.*

HOP TOAD

A cocktail made with apricot nectar liqueur and lemon juice, stirred with cracked ice and strained into a cocktail glass.

HORSE'S NECK (WITH A KICK)

A recipe straight from *Old Mr. Boston* (1935): Peel a rind of lemon in a spiral fashion and put it in a Collins glass with one end hanging over the rim. Fill the glass with ice cubes. Add a jigger of Old Mr. Boston rye or bourbon. Then fill with ginger ale and stir.

JACK ROSE

A classic cocktail made with applejack, lime juice, and grenadine. Shake with cracked ice and strain into a cocktail glass. For the literary among us, the Jack Rose appeared in Ernest Hemingway's 1926 novel *The Sun Also Rises*. Jake Barnes famously drinks a Jack Rose in a Paris hotel bar while waiting for Lady Brett Ashley. *Esquire.com*

JAMAICA GINGER

Also known as "Jake," Jamaica Ginger first became known in the nineteenth century as a medicinal extract, and then became infamous as a mixer during Prohibition. *Various sources.*

JELL-O SHOTS

Oddly enough, no recipe exists in the 1935 *Old Mr. Boston*. Let's just assume that the recipe has been lost to oblivion and move on.

LONE TREE

A cocktail made with Italian vermouth and dry gin that is shaken with cracked ice, strained into a cocktail glass, and served with a cherry and a twist.

LONG ISLAND ICED TEA

A relatively recent addition to the cocktail canon, this drink typically consists of four to five hard liquors and a splash of Coca-Cola. Ingredients may include tequila, rum, gin, vodka, and triple sec in equal—if not sloppy—amounts. *Various sources.*

MADEIRA

Madeira is a fortified Portuguese wine made in the Madeira Islands. The wine ranges from dry, which can be consumed as an aperitif, to sweet, which is typically served with dessert.

MAHARAJA'S REVENGE

Shake (Old Monk) rum, apricot brandy, and lime juice with ice and strain into a cocktail glass. *Created by Brother Cleve.*

MAIDEN'S BLUSH

A historic cocktail made with lemon juice, absinthe, grenadine, and dry gin. The cocktail can be traced back to nineteenth century France and resurfaced in the 1930 *Savoy Cocktail Book*, written by Harry Craddock.

MAMIE TAYLOR

Named for a famous turn-of-the twentieth century opera singer, this classic cocktail is made with Scotch, lime juice, ginger ale, ice, and served in a highball glass.

MANHATTAN

A well-known historic cocktail made with sweet Italian vermouth, rye or bourbon, bitters, and served with a cherry. *Various sources.*

MARY PICKFORD

Named for the famous actress of the early film era, this cocktail includes rum, vermouth, pineapple juice, grenadine, and Curaçao. It is shaken with cracked ice and strained into a Collins glass.

MEAD AND METHEGLIN

Mead is an ancient alcoholic beverage made with fermented honey and water. It can be light or rich, sweet or dry, sparkling or still. When herbs and spices are introduced, such as lavender or hops, the beverage is called Metheglin. *Various sources*

MINT JULEP

From the "smash" family of cocktails, the Mint Julep is most often made with bourbon, sugar, water and muddled mint. The drink is associated with the American South, and most specifically with Kentucky and the Kentucky Derby. *Various sources.*

MOSCOW MULE

A drink made with vodka, lime juice, and ginger beer. For the drink's history and discourse, refer to *Vintage Spirits & Forgotten Cocktails* by Ted Haigh.

NEGRONI

An aperitif made with gin, sweet vermouth and bitters (typically Campari). It is served in an old-fashioned or chilled cocktail glass with ice cubes and garnished with an orange slice. *Various sources.*

NEW ORLEANS FIZZ (OR RAMOS GIN FIZZ)

A drink created and made famous in New Orleans at the end of the nineteenth century, it's made with dry gin, lemon juice, powdered sugar, white of egg, sweet cream, orange flower, and mixed with soda water. It's a delight to behold—though one should only dare order such a libation at an appropriate establishment, where mixing a single drink that takes over ten to twelve minutes is acceptable. *Various sources.*

OLD FASHIONED

A drink made with rye or bourbon, sugar, bitters, and water, served over a large cube of ice and adorned with a slice of orange, a twist of lemon peel, and a cherry. Serve in Old Fashioned glass (that one is a no-brainer).

ORANGE BLOSSOM

A historic drink made with dry gin, fresh orange juice, and gum syrup. *Um...gum syrup?* Gum syrup is a sugar syrup incorporated with gum arabic, a resin from the Acacia tree. Today, most bartenders probably opt for a simple syrup, as gum syrup can be difficult to make—though purists might contend that gum syrup adds viscosity as well as sweetness.

PERIODISTA

A cocktail made with lime juice, sugar, apricot liqueur or apricot-flavored brandy, triple sec, either white or dark rum, and garnished with a twist of lime. *Various sources.* Interested readers should look at Devin Hahn's blog, "Periodista Tales" for variations and cocktail discourse.

PINK LADY

A cocktail made with dry gin, a dash or two of grenadine, applejack, and lemon juice, shaken with cracked ice and strained into a cocktail glass. Some variations call for a small amount of sweet or light cream and no applejack.

PINK SQUIRREL

A show-stopping drink made with crème de noyaux, crème de cacao, and heavy cream shaken with ice. Modern incarnations may call for blending the liqueurs with ice cream, in which case this pink creation should be served in a parfait glass. *Various sources.*

PLANTER'S PUNCH

A vaguely Caribbean, Tiki-style drink made with rum, grenadine, lemon, orange, lime, and pineapple juices.

PORTER

An extra-dark, strong ale.

PRESIDENTE

Or to be more accurate: *El Presidente.* This cocktail was created by an expat bartender in Havana during the thirsty stretch of American Prohibition. If you want to try it, and don't want to fly all the way to Havana (you would if you could, wouldn't you?) here's what you'll have to tell the guy behind the bar: light rum, dry vermouth, orange Curaçao, and fresh grenadine. Shake it in an iced cocktail shaker and strain. Serve in a cocktail glass. Garnish with a lemon twist and cherry. *Various sources.*

PUNCH

A precursor to the modern cocktail, punch has been popular in this country since before the Revolution. Simply put, there is a punch recipe for every party. We defer to David Wondrich's definition in his book, *Punch: The Delights and Dangers of the Flowing Bowl*: "It's not punch if there is nobody to drink it."

RICKEY

A rickey is a drink made of liquor (historically whiskey, now typically gin), lime or lemon juice, carbonated water, and ice.

ROB ROY

Named in honor of Henry Louis Reginald De Koven's operetta of the same name, a Rob Roy is a Manhattan made with whiskey instead of rye. Other ingredients include Italian vermouth and bitters stirred with cracked ice and strained into a cocktail glass.

SANGAREE

A sweet, chilled beverage made of wine or other alcoholic liquor and grated nutmeg. Those who are interested should investigate the copious recipes available in *How to Mix Drinks*, by Jerry Thomas, originally published in 1862.

SCREWDRIVER

Blame the 1980s: the screwdriver is a simple drink made with vodka and orange juice, and is sometimes considered to be a good hangover cure.

SEX ON THE BEACH

If you are able to order this cocktail without blushing, you will receive a drink made with vodka, peach schnapps, crème de cassis, orange juice, cranberry juice, and garnished with an orange slice and cherry. *Various sources.*

SHERRY COBBLER

Mentioned in Jerry Thomas's 1862 book, *How to Mix Drinks,* this cobbler includes sherry, sugar, and orange slices. It's shaken well and then garnished with berries in season, or with orange and pineapple slices.

SHERRY FLIP

A drink that was popular with nightclub drinkers in the 1940s, the Sherry Flip featured egg, powdered sugar, sherry, and cream. It was then shaken together and topped with freshly grated nutmeg.

SHRUB

A syrup that's prepared with fruit, sugar, and an acidic base, such as lemon juice or vinegar, then preserved. The aged syrup can then be mixed with spirits such as brandy or rum to make cocktails. *Various sources.*

SIDECAR

A cocktail made with lemon, Cointreau, and brandy shaken with cracked ice and strained into a cocktail glass with a sugared rim—an embellishment that puts the drink into a class of cocktails called a crusta. Ted Haigh writes about the interesting lineage of the Sidecar in his book *Vintage Spirits and Forgotten Cocktails.*

SILVER FIZZ

Part of a larger fizz family of cocktails, the Silver Fizz is made with lemon juice, powdered sugar, dry gin, and an egg white, and is then shaken with ice and strained into a glass, then topped with club soda. The egg white lends a gray or silver look to the drink.

SINGAPORE SLING

A tropical-styled drink from the 1930s, it is considered by some to be the prototype for the future "tiki" drink trends. Made with dry gin, cherry liqueur or cherry brandy, and Bénédictine, it is topped with seltzer water and garnished with fruit slices or the peel of a lemon or lime. See Ted Haigh's *Vintage Spirits and Forgotten Cocktails* for more information.

SMASH

A family of cocktails that begins with muddled (or "smashed") mint, the Smash has been around since at least the middle of the nineteenth century. As Jerry Thomas puts it in his 1862 book, *How to Mix Drinks*, "This beverage is simply a julep on a small plan."

STINGER

A drink that became popular in the middle of the twentieth century, the Stinger is made with white crème de menthe and brandy. It was often considered an appropriate "nightcap."

SWEET CATAWBA

A light, sweet, and fruity blush wine made from American grapes, this sweet wine was both mixed with spirits for cocktails and served on its own, particularly during the second half of the nineteenth century. *Various sources.*

TASSEL TOSSER

Though it is hard to imagine twirling this drink across one's palate, this cocktail, named for Sally Keith, Boston's most famous burlesque dancer, contains the following ingredients: brandy, anisette, and triple sec.

THE FORT POINT

A modern cocktail made with historic ingredients, from a modern bar that pays attention to the past, the Fort Point is made with rye whiskey, Punt e Mes, and Bénédictine, stirred with chipped ice and strained into a cocktail glass. It is served with a brandied cherry on the side. *Created by John Gertsen at Drink.*

TIMBER DOODLE

This recipe remains unknown today. Charles Dickens is said to have had a Timber Doodle—or at least remarked about it—on his 1842 visit to Boston: "There too the stranger is initiated into the mysteries of Gin-sling, Cocktail, Sangaree, Mint Julep, Sherry-cobbler, Timber Doodle, and other rare drinks."

TODDY

A drink that many think can fight the common cold, a toddy is made with liquor (typically whiskey or brandy), water, sugar, and sometimes spices. Toddies may be hot or cold. *Various sources.*

TOM AND JERRY

A somewhat complicated drink, the Tom and Jerry is made with eggs, sugar, rum, brandy, vanilla extract, allspice, cloves, cinnamon, milk, boiling water, and nutmeg. According to Jerry Thomas: "Beat the whites of the eggs to a stiff froth and the yolks until they are as thin as water. Then mix together and add the spice and rum. Thicken with sugar until the mixture attains the consistency of a light batter." Spoon the batter into a glass, adding brandy and boiling water. Grate fresh nutmeg on top. *Various sources, but purists should refer to Jerry Thomas's* How to Mix Drinks (1862).

TOM COLLINS

A ninetenth century drink made with dry gin, lemon juice and powdered sugar. The Tom Collins is served with several cubes of ice, filled with seltzer water, and garnished with a slice of lemon, a slice of orange, and a cherry.

VESPER MARTINI

Bond's preferred cocktail is made with dry gin, vodka, Kina Lillet, and a lemon peel. It is shaken in an iced cocktail shaker (not stirred) and strained into a stemmed cocktail glass. The martini is then garnished with the twist of a large lemon. *Various sources.*

WARD EIGHT

Said to have been created in Boston at the turn of the twentieth century, the Ward Eight is a classic cocktail with a somewhat mythical past. The drink is made with rye, lemon juice, orange juice, and grenadine. For specific recipes and the full story, see the introduction and conclusion of this book.

WHISKEY SMASH

One of the most popular cocktails from the "Smash" category, the Whiskey Smash is made with muddled mint, rye or bourbon, and served over ice cubes. The drink is then decorated with an orange slice, cherry, and a lemon peel twist and is served in an Old Fashioned glass.

WHISKEY SOUR

A simple cocktail made with rye or bourbon, a bit of sugar, and lemon juice, served over ice in a highball glass.

WHITE LADY

A drink made popular in the 1930s and 1940s, it was served at the Latin Quarter and other nightclubs around Boston. The White Lady is made with lemon juice, Cointreau, and dry gin and is served over cracked ice in a cocktail glass.

WOO WOO

Another 1980s cocktail using peach schnapps (see the Fuzzy Navel), the Woo Woo pairs the sweet liquor with vodka and cranberry juice. *Various sources.*

ZAZA

A turn of the twentieth century cocktail named for a popular play, the Zaza is made with dry gin, Dubonnet, and an orange peel.

ZOMBIE

A tropical-style drink that helped create the post-war "tiki" trend of the 1940s and 1950s, the Zombie was created by Don the Beachcomber at his Los Angeles bar in the 1930s. Made with white rum, golden rum, dark rum, lime juice, pineapple juice, papaya juice, and sugar, the Zombie earns the "two drink limit" that often comes along with it. *Esquire.com*

BIBLIOGRAPHY

Ade, George, *The Old-Time Saloon, Not Wet, Not Dry, Just History*, New York: Old Town Books, 1993

Ainley, Leslie G., *Boston Mahatma*, Boston: Bruce Humphries, Inc., 1949

Billings, John Shaw, Committee of Fifty, *The Liquor problem: a summary of investigations conducted by the Committee on Fifty, 1893-1903*, New York: Houghton, Mifflin, 1905

Bradford, Ned and Pam, *Boston's Locke-Ober Café*, New York: Atheneum, 1978

Burns, Eric, *The Spirits of America: A Social History of Alcohol*, Philadelphia: Temple University Press, 2004

Calkins, Raymond, Committee of Fifty for the Investigation of the Liquor Problem, *Substitutes for the saloon*, Houghton Mifflin Company, 1919

Clark, George Farber, *History of the temperance reform in Massachusetts, 1813-1883*, Clarke & Carruth, 1888

Connolly, James J., *The Triumph of Ethnic Progressivism: Urban Political Culture in Boston*, Boston: Harvard University Press, 1998

Conroy, David W., *In Public Houses, Drink and The Revolution of Authority in Colonial Massachusetts*, Chapel Hill: University of North Carolina Press, 1995

Conway, Lorie, *Boston The Way It Was*, Boston: WGBH Educational Foundation, 1996

Curtis, Wayne, *And a Bottle of Rum: A History of the New World in Ten Cocktails*, New York: Three Rivers Press, 2006, 2007

DeGroff, Dale, *The Craft of the Cocktail*, New York: Clarkson Potter, 2002

DeVoto, Bernard, *The Hour: A Cocktail Manifesto,* Tin House Books, 2010

Drake, Samuel Adams, *Old Boston Taverns and Tavern Clubs*, Boston: W. A. Butterfield, 1917 (First edition, Boston, 1886)

Duis, Perry, *The Saloon: Public Drinking in Chicago and Boston: 1880-1920*, Urbana and Chicago: University of Illinois Press, 1983

Earle, Alice Morse, *Stagecoach and Tavern Days*, New York: The Macmillan Company, 1900

Field, Edward, *The Colonial Tavern: A Glimpse of New England Town Life in the Seventeenth and Eighteenth Centuries*, Providence: Preston and Rounds, 1897

Fougner, G. Selmer, *Along the Wine Trail, Volume II*, reprinted from *The Sun*, New York, 1934.

Gately, Iain, *Drink: A Cultural History of Alcohol*, New York: Gotham Books, 2008

Grimes, William, *Straight Up or On the Rocks: the Story of the American Cocktail,* New York: North Point Press, 2001

Haigh, Ted, *Vintage Spirits and Forgotten Cocktails,* Beverly, Mass.: Quarry Books, 2009

Hale, James W., *Old Boston Town*, New York: Geo. F. Nesbitt, 1880

The History Project, foreword by Barney Frank, *Improper Bostonians: Lesbian and Gay History from the Puritans to Playland,* Boston: Beacon Press, 1998

Hobbes, Halliwell, *Latin Quarter Souvenir Book of Cocktails & How to Mix Them*, Restaurant Museum, 2008

Ingersoll, Joanne Dolan, *Cocktail Culture: Ritual and Invention in American Fashion, 1920-1980,* Museum of Art, Rhode Island School of Design, 2011

Kruh, David, *Always Something Doing: Boston's Infamous Scollay Square, Revised Edition*, Boston: Northeastern University Press, 1989, 1999

Miller, Neil, *Banned in Boston: The Watch and Ward Society's Crusade Against Books, Burlesque, and the Social Evil*, Boston: Beacon Press, 2011

Murdock, Catherine Gilbert, *Domesticating Drink: Women, Men, and Alcohol in America, 1870-1940*, Baltimore: Johns Hopkins University Press, 2001

Nash, Peter, *Boston's Royal Rooters*, Charleston, SC: Arcadia Publishing, 2005

Nathan, Gavin, *Historic Taverns of Boston*, Lincoln, Neb.: iUniverse, 2006

O'Connor, Thomas H., *The Boston Irish: A Political History*, Little, Brown, 1997

Okrent, Daniel, *Last Call: The Rise and Fall of Prohibition*, New York: Scribner, 2010

O'Neil, Luke, *Boston's Best Dive Bars: Drinking & Diving in Beantown*, Brooklyn: Gamble Guides, 2011

Oldenburg, Ray, *The Great Good Place: Cafés, Coffee Shops, Bookstores, Bars, Hair Salons, and Other Hangouts at the Heart of a Community*, Marlowe & Company, 1999

Powers, Madelon, *Faces Along the Bar: Lore and Order in the Workingman's Saloon: 1870 to 1920*, Chicago and London: The University of Chicago Press, 1998

Pozzetta, George, *Immigrant Institutions, the organization of immigrant life*, Routledge, 1991

Rorabaugh, W. J., *The Alcoholic Republic: An American Tradition*, Oxford: Oxford University Press, 1979

Salinger, Sharon V., *Taverns and Drinking in Early America*, Baltimore: Johns Hopkins University Press, 2004

Schiff, Pearl, *Scollay Square*, New York: Rinehart & Company, 1952

A Seidel for Jake Wirth, The Jacob Wirth Company, 1989

Sismondo, Christine, *America Walks Into a Bar: A Spirited History of Taverns and Saloons, Speakeasies and Grog Shops*, Oxford: Oxford University Press, 2011

Stoddard, Cora Frances, *Handbook of Modern Facts About Alcohol*, Boston: Scientific Temperance Federation, 1914

Sylvester, Robert, *No Cover Charge: A Backward Look at the Night Clubs*, New York: Dial Press, 1956

Thomas, Jerry, *How to Mix Drinks: or The Bon-vivant's Companion*, New York: Dick & Fitzgerald, 1862

Thwing, Anne Haven, *The Crooked & Narrow Streets of the Town of Boston 1630-1822*, Marshall Jones Company, 1920

Vacca, Richard, *The Boston Jazz Chronicles: Faces, Places and Nightlife, 1937-1962*, Belmont, Mass.: 2012

Walters, Barbara, *Audition: A Memoir*, New York: Knopf, 2008

Wondrich, David, *Imbibe! From Absinthe Cocktail to Whiskey Smash, a Salute in Stories and Drinks to "Professor" Jerry Thomas, Pioneer of the American Bar*, Perigee Trade, 2007

Woodbury, Marda Liggett, *Stopping The Presses: The Murder Of Walter W. Liggett*, University of Minnesota Press, 1998

Woods, Robert, *The City Wilderness: A Settlement Study*, Boston: Houghton Mifflin, 1898

Woods, Robert, *Americans in Process: A Settlement Study*, Boston: Houghton Mifflin, 1902

NOTES ON SOURCES

Introduction: Recipe for a Drinking Town

Interview with Lauren Clark in April 2012. Classic story of the Ward Eight based on Ned and Pam Bradford, *Boston's Locke-Ober Café*.

Taverns in Old Boston: The Spirit of Revolution

Information on the political and social nature of Boston's colonial-era taverns was largely based on David W. Conroy, *In Public Houses*, and W. J. Rorabaugh, *The Alcoholic Republic*. Details on names and locations of taverns and the price of liquor were largely based on the research by Samuel Adams Drake, *Old Boston Taverns and Tavern Clubs*, as well as Alice Morse Earle, *Stagecoach and Tavern Days*; Edward Field, *The Colonial Tavern*; Gavin Nathan, *Historic Taverns of Boston*; and *Taverns and Stagecoaches of New England*, Volume I and Volume II, State Street Trust Company, 1953. Details on the Boston Massacre were drawn from Hiller B. Zobel, *The Boston Massacre*, New York: Norton, 1970, p. 200, 206. Details on the Green Dragon from Nathaniel Shurtleff, *A Topographical and Historical Description of Boston*, Third Edition, Boston: Rockwell and Churchill, 1891, p. 605. Details on the life of Judge Sewall from his diary and Eve LaPlante, *Salem Witch Judge*, New York: HarperCollins, 2007.

Boston's Saloon History: Democracy on Tap

Information about nineteenth century drinking culture and habits in Boston bars were primarily drawn from two studies: Madelon Powers, *Faces Along the Bar*, and Perry Duis, *The Saloon: Public Drinking in Chicago and Boston*. Details on drinks and behavior in saloons came from George Ade, *The Old-Time Saloon*. Details on the number of Boston bars from John Shaw Billings of the Committee of Fifty report on *The Liquor Problem*. Per capita drinking rates from Otto L. Bettman, *The Good Old Days: They Were Terrible*, New York: Random House, 1974, p. 129. The pig story is from Clark, *History of the temperance reform in Massachusetts,* p. 43. Details on drinking among Irish, Italians, African-Americans, and other groups in the South End and other neighborhood came in large part from two studies, edited by Robert Woods, *The City Wilderness: A Settlement Study* and *Americans in Process: A Settlement Study,* Boston. Other details on immigrant bars came from Duis, Powers, and George Pozzetta, *Immigrant Institutions, the organization of immigrant life.* Charles Dickens's description of drinks was from *American Notes for General Circulation,* Baudry's European Library, 1842, p. 71; Nathaniel Hawthorne's Parker House description is from *Passages from the American Note-Books,* May 7, 1850, Boston: Houghton Mifflin, 1868, p. 476-494. Details about Jacob Wirth are largely drawn from *A Seidel for Jake Wirth,* and articles in the *Boston Globe,* including Wirth's obituary on December 13, 1965. Information on the Bell in Hand Tavern is based on the account by the Rev. Edward G. Porter in *Rambles in Old Boston, New England,* Cupples, Upham and Company, 1886, p. 357-360, as well as Edmund Monroe Bacon, *Bacon's Dictionary of Boston,* 1886, p. 39 with additional details from Paul Douglas Shand-Tucci, *Boston Bohemia 1881- 1900: Ralph Adams Cram: Life and Architecture,* University of Massachusetts Press, 1995, p. 54. Details on P.J. Kennedy from Lawrence Leamer, *The Kennedy Men, 1901-1963,* New York: Morrow, 2001, p. 4-5; and John Davis, *The Kennedys: Dynasty and Disaster,* SPI Books, 1993, p. 34; Information on "Nuf Ced" McGreevey was drawn from articles and ephemera in McGreevey Scrapbook held at the Boston Public Library, and Peter Nash, *Boston's Royal Rooters.*

Prohibition, Parts I-IV

The history of the temperance movement in New England and the lead up to Prohibition is based largely on George Farber Clark, *History of the temperance reform in Massachusetts,* as well as Daniel Okrent, *Last Call;* Rorabaugh, *The Alcohol Republic;* and Edward Behr, *Prohibition: 13 Years that Changed America,* New York Arcade, 1996. Insight into temperance politics was also provided by Dio Lewis, *Prohibition a failure: or, The true solution of the temperance question,* Boston: 1875. Information on Mary Hanchett Hunt and Cora Frances Stoddard came from "Scientific Temperance Federation, 1881-1934" by Laurel G. Bowen, and "The Temperance and Prohibition Movement in America 1830-

1933," by Randall C. Jimerson, which were contained in the *Guide to Microfilm Edition of Temperance and Prohibition Papers* published by the University of Michigan in 1977. This massive microtext collection, a copy of which is at the Boston Public Library, provided key details on the work of Hunt and Stoddard; it also contains the personal files and raw research notes from Stoddard. Other information on Hunt and Stoddard from David J. Hansen's articles posted on "Alcohol: Problems and Solutions" at www2.potsdam.edu/hansondj/Controversies/Biography-Mary-H-Hunt.html and www2.potsdam.edu/hansondj/Controversies/Biography-Cora-F-Stoddard.html. Other information on Stoddard came from the Summer 1936, memorial edition of the *Scientific Temperance Journal*, which was devoted to her life, as well as her publications on alcohol use, such as *Handbook of Modern Facts about Alcohol*, published in 1914, and articles like "How Prohibition Came to the United States," published in the October 1919 issue of *Social Hygiene*. Details on Boston speakeasies were found in stories from *Boston Herald, Boston Globe,* and other contemporary publications. Details on the "scofflaw" contest found in *Boston Globe*, January 16, and February 29, 1924, and *Boston Herald* on January 16, 1924. Details on the life of Charles Solomon come from Schorow and Beverly Ford, *The Boston Mob Guide*, History Press, 2011, as well as stories by Austen Lake in the *Boston Evening American* and other newspaper accounts. Details on Walter Liggett were found in his daughter's account of his life, *Stopping the Presses,* as well as "Bawdy Boston" in *Plain Talk*, January 1930. Details on Oliver Garrett were from "Bawdy Boston," and numerous articles in the *Boston Globe;* in particular, see: "Garrett Gives Up to Post," July 11, 1957, and "Ask the Globe," January 3, 1988. The story of James Sheehan was based on interview with his son William Sheehan, February 2012, as well as "First Class," by William G. Brooks and Margaret Sullivan, *FBI National Academy Associates Magazine*, September/October 2011.

The Conga Belt: Nightclubs in Boston

Information on Boston's nightclubs is based on interviews with Edith Nussinow, January and April 2012, Rose Arntz and Ronald Arntz, October, 2011. For a description of the Latin Quarter, I relied heavily on Barbara Walters's memoir, *Audition,* as well as Robert Sylvester, *No Cover Charge,* and Laurie Cabot interview, February, 2012. I also relied on the nightclub column "Spilling the Beans" by Joseph Dinneen in the *Boston Globe* and articles by William Buchanan, *Boston Globe*. Background on Boston's jazz clubs are based on interviews with Ron Della Chiesa, June 2012, Sarah-Ann Shaw, July 2012, and Connie Dodge, February 2011, as well as Richard Vacca, *The Boston Jazz Chronicles,* and "Connelly's Bar," a 1997 report from Boston Landmarks Commission. Information from Blinstrub's Village came from interviews with Heidi Webb and Adele Maestranzi, March 2012, and material posted on "The Life and Times of Stanley Blinstrub and the Famous Blinstrub's Nightclub," by Mike McGoff, http://blinstrubas.com/blinstrubsclub/blinstrubs.htm and "Hubscapes, Blinstrub's" produced by Boston Neighborhood Network, February 12, 2008. Details on the Blinstrub fire from "Memories of Show Greats Linger," Ernie Santosuosso, *Boston Globe*, February 8, 1968.

Boston's Brewing Past

This chapter relied heavily on information provided by researcher Michael Reiskind of Jamaica Plain including an interview in June 2012, and material compiled and posted by the Jamaica Plain Historical Society, www.jphs.org. Other sources include "The Ale Trail," by Mike Miliard, *The Boston Phoenix,* May 27-June 2, 2005; "Boston's Beer-Making Past," Michael Reiskind, Boston.com, November 29, 2010; Josh B. Wardrop, "Beer Masters," Boston Guide, *Panorama Magazine,* October 24, 2005; *Documentary History of the United States Brewers; Association, Part I,* New York: United States Brewers' Association, 1896; "The Rise of the Beer Barons," by Carl H. Miller, *All About Beer Magazine,* 1999, cited by www.beerhistory.com; and Edmund Monroe Bacon, *Bacon's Dictionary of Boston,* p. 40-42. Other information was found in 1912 editions of *Western Brewer and Journal of the Barley, Malt and Hop Trades.* Details on August E. Haffenreffer, his family, and the beer's reputation were from his obituary, *Boston Globe,* August 30, 2010. Information on breweries in other parts of Boston from Peter F. Stevens, *Hidden History of the Boston Irish,* The History Press, 2008, and Nathan, *Historic Taverns of Boston.*

Neighborhood Bars: Boston's Home Away from Home

This chapter was based on interviews with Eddie Burke, May 2011, Jerry Burke, May 2012, Jerry Foley, April 2012, Brother Cleve, March 2012, Sarah-Ann Shaw, July 2012, Patrick Sullivan, March 2012, and Jamie Sullivan, March 2012, as well as articles in the *Boston Herald* and *Boston Globe*, including "Taking a Stroll Through History," Alan Lupo, *Boston Globe*, July 19, 1992. Information on the Warren Tavern from James F. Hunnewell's history of Charlestown, *A Century of Town Life*, Charlestown, First Church, 1888. Details about Scollay Square were from interview with David Kruh, April 2012, and his book, *Always Something Doing*. Information on gay bars provided in interviews with Robert David Sullivan, May 2012, Leo Motsis, Roger Sampson, and Eagle Bar patrons, June 2012, Libby Bouvier, July 2012, and from ephemera, clips, and photos at the History Project. Also see "Last Call" by Sullivan, *Boston Globe*, December 2, 2007. Details on Jimmy O'Keefe based on interview with Ed Corsetti in 2003 and from Mike Barnicle column in the *Globe*, August 2, 1987, and *Globe*, July 28, 1987. Material on Reagan and the Eire pub based on reporting by *Globe* writers John Powers on January 28, 1983, and Kevin Cullen, January 25, 1983 and May 2, 2008. Details on the Littlest Bar from *Boston Herald*, September 19, 2003. Other information came from O'Neil's *Boston Best Dive Bars*, Oldenburg's *The Great Good Place*, and "When Last Call Was Not an Issue," by Dick Sinnott, *Boston Globe*, November 7, 1990.

Revolution in a Cocktail Glass

Background on the origin of the word cocktail from DeGroff, *The Craft of the Cocktail*. Information on Boston craft cocktails came largely from numerous interviews and e-mails in 2011 and 2012 with Brother Cleve, Jackson Cannon, Misty Kalkofen, Jamie Walsh, Alexei Beratis, Jamie Walsh, Lauren Clark, and John Gertsen. Other sources included the "Meet Your Bartender" series by Susanna Bolle, for National Public Radio Kitchen, which included Gertsen (August 20, 2010), Cannon (November 30, 2010), Cleve (June 15, 2011), and Kalkofen (January 3, 2011), www.publicradiokitchen.wbur.org. Of great help was the "Craft Cocktail Section" in the *Boston Globe*, February 15, 2012, which included "Cocktail Creationists," by Luke O'Neil, "How

About a Cocktail?" by Devra First, and "Make it an Old-Fashioned," by Jim Chiavelli. Other sources include "Mixing Music and Cocktails," by O'Neil, *Boston Globe*, March 17, 2011; and "Ghosts of Hangovers Past," Giglio, *Boston Magazine*, February 2008. Details on Old Mr. Boston distillery from "Looking for Mr. Boston," Joshua Glenn, *Boston Globe*, December 28, 2003. Other sources: "She Drank 17 'Milk Shakes,'" *Boston Globe*, August 5, 1934, and DeVoto, *The Hour: A Cocktail Manifesto*.

Conclusion: The Mystery of the Ward Eight

Classic story of the Ward Eight based on the Bradfords' *Boston's Locke-Ober Café*. Other key details are from "There's More than Beans to Boston: The Hub City's legendary Locke-Ober's is one of America's great restaurants," by George Frazier, *Holiday Magazine*, January, 1951; Fougner's *Along the Wine Trail*, p. 102; Wondrich, *Imbibe*; "Ten Best Cocktails of 1934," Frank Shay, *Esquire*, December 1934; and handouts from Locke-Ober and Drink. Details on the life of Martin Lomasney are from Ainley's *Boston Mahatma*; "The Lomasney Legend," by Albert D. Van Nostrand, *The New England Quarterly*, Vol. 21, No. 4, December 1948, p. 435-458; "Martin Lomasney as I Knew Him," B. Loring Young, *Proceedings of the Massachusetts Historical Society*, Third Series, Vol. 75, (1963) p. 52-65; "Martin Lomasney: The Story of His Life, As Related by Him to Thomas Carens," *Boston Herald*, December 2 to December 21, 1925; and items in the Martin M. Lomasney Scrapbooks, 1902-1932, Massachusetts Historical Society. Sources on "The Great Ward Eight Debate" include interviews with Cannon, Kalkofen, and Gertsen, as well as "Bar Association," Anthony Giglio, *Boston Magazine*, March 2006.

Courtesy the Collection of Kathy Alpert/Postmark Press.

INDEX

H

I

J

Reagan, Ronald, 192-93

Red Hat, The, 183

Red Lion, 27, 37

Red Sox Ale, 161

Redstone, Michael, 146

Reiskind, Michael, 157-59, 163, 167-68

Renard, Jacques, 106, 131, 135-37

Repeal night, 125-27

Revere Brewery, 159

Revere House, 230

Revere, Paul, 39, 41, 168, 177, 236

Richardson, Thomas "Sandy," 92

Romney, Mitt, 173

Rorabaugh, W.J., 27, 49, 78
  Alcoholic Republic, The, 27, 49

Roslindale, 159

Rourke, Daniel, 238-39

Roxbury, 70, 149, 159, 176, 212

Roxbury Crossing, 159

Royal Exchange, 27, 34, 36

Royal Rooters, 71-72, 203

Royale Marshals band, 141

Rueter Company, 160, 163-64, 167

Rush, Benjamin, 78, 86

Russell, Bill, 176

Ruth, Babe, 163

S

Saints, 197

Salem witchcraft trials, 33

Salutation Tavern, 27, 37, 41

Sampson, Roger, 194-95

Samuel Adams beer (see also
  Boston Beer Company – Jamaica
  Plain), 157, 167-68, 187

Santa Clara Co., 234

Santosuosso, Ernie, 154

Schiff, Pearl, 181

Schlitz, 54, 160

Scientific Temperance Association, 85

Scientific Temperance
  Federation, 86, 113

Scollay Square, 27, 133, 181-85,
  196, 203

Sedgewick, Robert, 158

Sewall, Samuel, 33-36, 66

Shay, Frank, 232, 242

Shaw, Sarah-Ann, 149, 176

Sheehan, James, 119

Sheehan, William, 119

Ship Tavern, 27

Silvertone, 131, 221

Slades Bar and Grill, 176

Solmonte, Vincent, 190

Solomon, Bertha, 111, 107

Solomon, Charles, 103-12, 116,
  137, 141, 144

Somewhere Else, 197

Sons of Liberty, 39-40

South Boston, 17, 54, 91-92, 111,
  120, 134, 151-54, 159-60, 164,
  167-68, 174-77, 180, 191, 202, 209

South End, 49, 65, 103, 109, 118,
  133-35, 147-49, 171-73, 175-76,
  178, 180, 196, 199, 204

V

W

ABOUT THE AUTHOR

Stephanie Schorow learned to write with a hangover during her many years as a reporter and editor for the *Boston Herald*, the Associated Press, the *Stamford Advocate* and other newspapers around the country. She is the author of six books about Boston history and teaches both writing and pottery. She shares her Medford home with 2½ cats.

www.stephanieschorow.com

ABOUT THE DESIGNER

Holly Gordon is a freelance graphic artist who grew up on Boston's North Shore. After graduating from The New England Institute of Art, she dove into an independent career and has worked on a wide range of illustrative projects. She has moved cross country twice in one year and is currently settled in Cambridge.

See her work online at www.missgordon.com

ABOUT THE PUBLISHER

Union Park Press is an independent publisher specializing in books about the arts, history, and culture of Boston and New England. Our goal is to bring these cultural riches to life with sophisticated, in-depth writing and a fresh, contemporary point of view.

For more about who we are and what we do, visit us online at www.unionparkpress.com